WALCH EDUCAT

W9-ATR-954

16 MORE ^ Extraordinary Hispanic Americans

Nancy Lobb

930
Lab
c.1
2010

15.35

PHOTO CREDITS

Franklin Chang-Díaz	Courtesy of NASA
Joseph Unanue	© 2009 Dario Acosta
Guy Gabaldon	Courtesy of Ohana Gabaldon, AP Images
Nicholasa Mohr	Courtesy of Catherine Balkin
Isabel Allende	© 2008 Lori Barra
Mario Molina	Donna Coveney/MIT
Bill Richardson	© 2009 Alexandre Meneghini, AP Images
Carlos Santana	© 2000 Steffen Schmidt, AP Images
Antonia Hernandez	Courtesy of CA Community Foundation
Gloria Estefan	© 2008 Dan Steinberg, AP Images
Edgar Prado	Adam Coglianese, Courtesy of NYRA
Salma Hayek	© 2006 Paul White, AP Images
Christy Turlington	© 2004 Jennifer Graylock, AP Images
Rebecca Lobo	© 1997 Bob Galbraith, AP Image
Alex Rodriguez	© 2007 Kathy Willens, AP Images
Scott Gomez	© 2008 Mary Altaffer, AP Images

1   2   3   4   5   6   7   8   9   10
ISBN 978-0-8251-6503-0
Copyright © 2009
J. Weston Walch, Publisher
40 Walch Drive • Portland, ME 04103
www.walch.com
Printed in the United States of America

WALCH EDUCATION®

Contents

To the Teacher

According to *Reading Next: A Vision for Action and Research in Middle and High School Literacy*, a report to the Carnegie Corporation of New York (2004, second edition), "High-interest, low-difficulty texts play a significant role in an adolescent literacy program and are critical for fostering the reading skills of struggling readers and the engagement of all students. In addition to using appropriate grade-level textbooks that may already be available in the classroom, it is crucial to have a range of texts in the classroom that link to multiple ability levels and connect to students' background experiences."

Biographies about extraordinary people are examples of one such kind of text. The 16 Americans described in this collection should both inspire and reassure students. As students read, your instruction can include approaches that will support not only comprehension, but also learning from passages.

Reading and language arts skills not only enrich students' academic lives but also their personal lives. The *Extraordinary Americans* series was written to help students gain confidence as readers. The biographies were written to pique students' interest while engaging their understanding of vocabulary, recalling facts, identifying the main idea, drawing conclusions, and applying knowledge. The added value of reading these biographies is that students will learn about other people and, perhaps, about themselves.

Students will read stories demonstrating that great things are accomplished by everyday people who may have grown up just like them—or maybe even with greater obstacles to overcome. Students will discover that being open to new ideas, working hard, and believing in one's self make them extraordinary people, too!

Structure of the Book

The Biographies

This collection of stories can be used in many different ways. You may assign passages for independent reading or engage students in choral reading. No matter which strategies you use, each passage contains pages to guide your instruction.

At the end of each passage, you will find a series of questions. The questions are categorized, and you can assign as many as you wish. The purposes of the questions vary:

- **Remembering the Facts:** Questions in this section engage students in a direct comprehension strategy, and require them to recall and find information while keeping track of their own understanding.

- **Understanding the Story:** Questions posed in this section require a higher level of thinking. Students are asked to draw conclusions and make inferences.

- **Getting the Main Idea:** Once again, students are able to stretch their thinking. Questions in this section are fodder for dialog and discussion around the extraordinary individuals and important points in their lives.

- **Applying What You've Learned:** Proficient readers internalize and use the knowledge that they gain after reading. The question or activity posed allows students to connect what they have read to their own lives.

In the latter part of the book, there are additional resources to support your instruction.

Vocabulary

A list of key words is included for each biography. The lists can be used in many ways. Assign words for students to define, use them for spelling lessons, and so forth.

Answer Key

An answer key is provided. Responses will likely vary for Getting the Main Idea and Applying What You've Learned questions.

Additional Activities

Extend and enhance students' learning! These suggestions include conducting research, creating visual art, exploring cross-curricular activities, and more.

References

Learn more about each extraordinary person, or assign students to discover more on their own. Start with the sources provided.

To the Student

The lives of many Hispanic Americans have made a difference in the story of America. Writers, artists, scientists, teachers, politicians, ministers, lawyers, doctors, businesspeople, athletes, and so many more have helped to make the United States what it is today. Hispanic Americans can be proud of their heritage. It is a pride all Americans should share.

In *16 Extraordinary Hispanic Americans*, you read the stories of sixteen of these people. In *16 MORE Extraordinary Hispanic Americans,* you will read the stories of sixteen more outstanding Hispanic Americans. They are:

- Franklin Chang-Díaz, a rocket scientist who was the first Hispanic-American astronaut

- Joseph Unanue, a business leader who built Goya Foods into the largest Hispanic-owned company in the United States

- Guy Gabaldon, a U.S. Marine who captured 1,500 Japanese soldiers by himself during the Battle of Saipan in World War II

- Nicholasa Mohr, an artist and author of novels and short stories for young adults

- Isabel Allende, one of the first successful Hispanic-American female novelists

- Mario Molina, winner of the Nobel Prize in chemistry for discovering that CFCs were destroying the ozone layer

- Bill Richardson, a U.S. politician who has been nominated for the Nobel Peace Prize five times

- Carlos Santana, a famous guitarist who is known for his humanitarian work

- Antonia Hernandez, a lawyer who has worked hard for Hispanic civil rights

- Gloria Estefan, a singer who is known as the Queen of Latin Pop

- Edgar Prado, a jockey best known for his work with the beloved racehorse Barbaro

- Salma Hayek, an actress and producer who has worked hard for charities

- Christy Turlington, an American supermodel who has used her fame to help others

- Rebecca Lobo, a women's basketball player and Olympic gold-medalist whose successes helped lead to the creation of the WNBA

- Alex Rodriguez, a baseball player who was the youngest player ever to hit 500 home runs

- Scott Gomez, the first Hispanic-American National Hockey League player

The motto on the Great Seal of the United States reads "E PLURIBUS UNUM." That is Latin for "Out of many, one." The United States is made up of many peoples of many ethnic backgrounds. These peoples have come together to form one nation. Each group has been an important part of American history. I hope you will enjoy reading about sixteen Hispanic Americans who have made a difference.

—Nancy Lobb

Franklin Chang-Díaz
Astronaut

Franklin Chang-Díaz was the first Hispanic-American astronaut. He flew seven missions on U.S. space shuttles. This tied the record for most missions flown by one astronaut.

Chang-Díaz is also a rocket scientist. His work focuses on plasma propulsion technology. Someday, his rocket engines may allow manned space flights to other planets.

Franklin Chang-Díaz was born on April 5, 1950, in San José, Costa Rica. His father, Ramón Chang, was a construction worker. He was a Costa Rican of Chinese descent. Ramón married María Díaz, also of Costa Rica. The couple had six children.

On October 4, 1957, María Díaz told seven-year-old Franklin that there was a new star in the sky. It was the satellite *Sputnik*. It had just been launched by the Soviet Union. It was the first human-made satellite in space.

Franklin was fascinated. He decided that someday he would travel to space. Day after day, he and his cousins played astronauts in the backyard. An empty cardboard box became their spaceship.

Franklin wrote a letter in Spanish to the well-known rocket scientist, Wernher von Braun. He asked von Braun how to become an astronaut. The scientist wrote back. He told Franklin to study math and science. He said Franklin should learn to speak English. He advised him to study in the United States.

When there were space flights, Franklin listened to the radio broadcasts. He heard Houston mission control. He heard the astronauts on the Mercury and Gemini flights. He later said, "I knew the names of all the astronauts. But I thought, 'Who is this guy Roger? Boy, this guy is lucky. He gets to go on all the flights.' "

In high school, Franklin read a NASA brochure. (NASA is the National Aeronautics and Space Administration.) It was called "So You Want to Be a Rocket Scientist." He wrote a letter to NASA for more information. He was told that only United States citizens could become astronauts.

This did not discourage Franklin. He decided to go to the United States after he graduated from high school in 1967. He later said, "After high school, I got a job in a bank to save money. I told everyone that I was going to go to the United States to become a rocket scientist and an astronaut. Everyone laughed!"

Franklin's father didn't laugh. He bought his son a one-way ticket to the United States. Franklin arrived with the $50 he had saved from his job at the bank. He lived with an uncle in Connecticut.

Franklin repeated his senior year of high school at Hartford High School. He learned to speak English. He graduated in 1969. He won a four-year scholarship to the University of Connecticut. Franklin started college the same year that Neil Armstrong landed and walked on the moon.

When Franklin arrived to start class, there was a big problem. The university had realized Franklin was not a U.S. citizen. They had confused Costa Rica with Puerto Rico. Puerto Ricans are U.S. citizens. Costa Ricans are not. Therefore, Franklin was not eligible for the scholarship that he had won after all. He did not get the four-year scholarship. But the school did give him a one-year scholarship.

To pay his expenses, Franklin got a job. He became a research assistant in the physics lab. He was part of a team that worked with high-energy atomic collisions. He later said, "How's that for luck? That was one of the most American things that ever happened to me. Here there's a mind-set that if you work hard, you usually get what you want. It's still a land of opportunity."

Franklin found another challenge to becoming an astronaut. At that time, all astronauts were in the military. He could not join the military because he was not a U.S. citizen. He hoped that in the future, scientists would be astronauts, too. So, he studied engineering and physics.

He knew that his chances of becoming an astronaut were slim. He wanted to love his career even if he never reached his goal. Franklin followed his passion to build rockets.

Franklin earned his college degree in mechanical engineering in 1973. In 1977, he became a doctor of applied plasma physics. He earned this degree at MIT (Massachusetts Institute of Technology). At MIT, he worked on the design and function of fusion reactors.

Franklin Chang-Díaz began working at the Charles Stark Draper Laboratory at MIT in 1977. That same year, he became a U.S. citizen.

By this time, scientists were being recruited as astronauts. Chang-Díaz applied for the space-shuttle program. NASA asked him to come to Houston for interviews and tests. This was the first time a naturalized citizen had been considered as an astronaut. (A naturalized citizen is a person who was not born in the United States but then met the legal rules to become a U.S. citizen.)

Months went by. Chang-Díaz heard nothing more from NASA. He was not surprised. There had been 3,000 applicants for only 19 slots.

Then in 1980, he got a call from NASA. The caller wondered if he would be interested in becoming an astronaut! Chang-Díaz was amazed that anyone would ask him that question. He had dreamed of this moment since he was seven years old.

Chang-Díaz began his training in August 1981. At first, he worked on mission support teams. On January 12, 1986, he flew his first mission on the space shuttle *Columbia*. The mission lasted six days. In that time, the shuttle orbited Earth 96 times.

On this flight, Chang-Díaz helped launch a satellite. He did experiments in astrophysics. He also ran the materials processing lab.

Chang-Díaz said he had strong feelings on his first flight. "When you get to space, you want to do two things. You want to unstrap, because even though you train for zero gravity, you never know exactly what it's like until you're in it. The second thing you want to do is look out the window. That's what blows you away—to see Earth from that point. I've flown many times now, and the feeling is always the same."

Chang-Díaz's second flight was on the space shuttle *Atlantis*. The launch took place on October 18, 1989. Chang-Díaz worked on mapping the ozone in Earth's atmosphere. He also helped deploy the spacecraft *Galileo*. Its mission was to explore the planet Jupiter.

In 1992, Chang-Díaz flew aboard *Atlantis* again. On this mission, the crew tested the first Tethered Satellite System (TSS). They also launched the European Retrievable Carrier satellite.

In 1994, Chang-Díaz flew his fourth mission. This flight was on the space shuttle *Discovery*. The crew of this mission was the first to include a Russian cosmonaut (astronaut).

Chang-Díaz's fifth flight was in 1996 on *Columbia*. On this flight, the crew did many more TSS experiments. In one, they showed the ability of tethers to produce electricity.

In 1998, Chang-Díaz flew again on *Discovery*. This flight was the ninth and last docking of a U.S. space shuttle with the Russian space station Mir. (The word *mir* means "peace.") Cosmonauts and astronauts lived and worked at Mir for up to a year at a time. Space shuttles brought supplies and trade-off crew members.

This *Discovery* flight ended the first phase of the joint U.S.-Russian space shuttle program. Eleven space shuttle flights had docked with Mir between December 1994 and June 1998.

After 15 years in space, the Mir space station was wearing out. Russia did not have the money for the expensive repairs. In the end, Russia guided Mir back to Earth. On March 23, 2001, Mir plunged into the Pacific Ocean.

By this time, the International Space Station (ISS) was being built. Many countries and private companies worked together to build it. Space shuttles ferried crews, supplies, and building materials to the ISS.

Chang-Díaz's seventh flight launched on June 5, 2002. The *Endeavour* delivered a fresh crew for the ISS. They repaired the station's robot arm. Chang-Díaz did three space walks. On these walks, he helped install a mobile base for operating the robotic arm. With this flight, he tied the record for most space flights by an astronaut. In all, Chang-Díaz had logged more than 1,600 hours in space.

On each space flight, Chang-Díaz wore a watch set to Houston time. That is where he lived with his wife, Peggy, and four daughters. It's also where he worked when he was not flying. He was director of the Advanced Space Propulsion Laboratory at NASA from 1993 to 2005.

Being an astronaut is a risky job. Franklin Chang-Díaz had two narrow escapes in his career. He was first assigned to the 1986 flight of the space shuttle *Challenger*. But NASA moved him and his crew to an earlier flight on *Columbia*. That was lucky for him. *Challenger* exploded shortly after liftoff. Everyone aboard died.

In 2003, the space shuttle *Columbia* broke up during re-entry. All of the crew died. Franklin Chang-Díaz had flown just two flights before this tragedy.

Franklin Chang-Díaz retired from NASA in 2005. He is now president and chief executive officer of Ad Astra Rocket Company (AARC). AARC's mission is the development of a new kind of rocket technology. It is called the Variable Specific Impulse Magnetoplasma Rocket (VASIMR).

Chang-Díaz has been working on this concept since 1979. He began his work on this idea at the Charles Stark Draper Lab at MIT. He continued at the MIT Plasma Fusion Center. Then he moved this work to NASA's Johnson Space Center in 1994. Today, he continues his work at AARC.

The VASIMR engine would make travel between planets faster. VASIMR would also be able to drive cargo missions with very large payloads (more than 100 tons) to other planets.

The VASIMR engine works differently than traditional rocket engines do. Chang-Díaz uses hydrogen gas to generate enormous heat. Radio waves cause the hydrogen atoms to lose electrons. This changes them into plasma. Plasma reaches 50,000°F and higher. It is so hot it burns through any material known to human beings.

The only way plasma can be controlled is by using magnetic fields. Chang-Díaz has developed a system of magnetic fields shaped like the nozzle of a rocket. The plasma energy flows through the fields to power the rocket. It is kept inside the fields. It does not melt the rocket. Chang-Díaz has said the system is similar to a microwave oven.

The goal of this research is simple. Chang-Díaz hopes his engine will someday be used to power a rocket to Mars or beyond. When it does, he hopes to be aboard.

Chang-Díaz works to help young people succeed in science. He recruits graduate students from all over the world to work in his lab. He also supports space programs in Latin America. A branch of his company AARC opened in Costa Rica in 2005.

In his native Costa Rica, Franklin Chang-Díaz is a hero. Every schoolchild knows his name. A stamp was recently released in his honor. A scientist named a new species of rain forest beetle after Chang-Díaz. In 1995, Costa Rica made him an "Honorary Citizen." This is a very high honor!

Franklin Chang-Díaz has achieved his boyhood dream of becoming an astronaut and rocket scientist. He says, "It has been a wonderful 25 years. I've flown seven missions. I've done just about anything that there is to do in space."

Remembering the Facts

1. What sparked Franklin's interest in space travel when he was young?

2. How did Franklin pay for his college expenses?

3. What two things did Franklin Chang-Díaz want to do on his first space flight?

4. What was Mir?

5. What spacecraft did Chang-Díaz deploy on the space shuttle *Atlantis*?

6. What record did Chang-Díaz set on the 2002 flight of *Endeavour*?

7. What is AARC?

8. What are the two advantages of VASIMR over traditional rocket technology?

Understanding the Story

9. When Franklin lost his scholarship and took a job in the physics lab to pay his expenses, he said, "That was one of the most American things that ever happened to me."

    What do you think he meant by this?

10. Why do you think Chang-Díaz is a hero in his native Costa Rica?

Getting the Main Idea

In what ways do you think Franklin Chang-Díaz is a good role model for young Americans?

Applying What You've Learned

Imagine you are looking at Earth from a vantage point in space. How do you think you would feel? Write a paragraph or poem, or draw a picture, that expresses the emotions you think you would feel.

Joseph Unanue
Business Leader

Joseph Unanue was president of Goya Foods for 27 years. He built Goya into the largest Hispanic-owned company in the United States. Goya began as an importer of olive oil and sardines. Today, it sells 1,600 Hispanic food products nationwide. Its sales are more than $1 billion per year.

Goya has given to dozens of worthy causes. The company has a long history of quick response in times of disasters. When hurricanes or other disasters struck Florida, Mexico, and other areas, trucks filled with Goya foods quickly rolled south. Joseph Unanue said, "It is of great importance that Goya answer the call in time of need."

Joseph Unanue was born on March 14, 1925, in Brooklyn, New York. He was the second of four boys.

Joseph's father, Prudencio Unanue Ortiz, was born in Spain. At 16, he moved to Puerto Rico. There he met Carolina Casal. Her family had also come to Puerto Rico from Spain.

Prudencio moved to Brooklyn, New York, for a while. But he was in love with Carolina. He went back to Puerto Rico for her. The couple married in 1921. Soon afterward, they moved back to Brooklyn. They eventually had four sons.

Prudencio missed the tastes and smells of foods from "the old country." So, he opened a small business in 1928 importing foods from

Spain. Many Spanish immigrants lived in Manhattan. They loved being able to get traditional Spanish foods, such as olives, olive oil, and sardines.

But in the 1930s, the Spanish Civil War began. Prudencio's supplies were cut off. He began importing sardines from Morocco. In 1936, he bought the rights to the Goya name for $1. He chose the name because he thought it was easier to pronounce than his own name.

During the summers, Joseph and some of his brothers worked in the family business. Joseph started working when he was 14. His job was packing olives. He was paid $1 a day. He used most of his pay just to get to work. He had to catch a train and ferry boat to get there and back.

In 1943, Joseph graduated from St. Cecilia's High School in New Jersey. After graduation, he took a vacation. When he came home, he found a draft notice waiting for him. World War II was raging. More soldiers were needed.

After basic training, Joseph Unanue was sent to the European front. His company landed in France in December 1944. They joined General George S. Patton's 3rd Army at the Battle of the Bulge.

Within ten days, half of Unanue's army company was out of action. Some were wounded. Some had frostbite. Others died. His sergeant was killed. Unanue was offered a promotion to sergeant. He turned down the offer because he didn't feel ready. His friend was promoted instead. Unanue said, "He was a guy who really deserved it."

Unanue kept his rank of private first class. But still, he was a natural leader. He pulled his men to safety during intense German shelling. For his bravery, Unanue was awarded the Bronze Star.

In 1946, after the war ended, Unanue returned home. He enrolled in Catholic University of America under the GI Bill. This benefit paid for veterans to attend college. He earned a degree in mechanical engineering.

After college, Unanue looked for work. He turned down his first job offer. He said, "I thought I should be making more money than they offered. So, I went to work for my father for half the price." Joseph's brothers, Tony and Frank Unanue, also joined the family business.

After World War II, many people immigrated to the United States. Puerto Ricans came looking for work. The Unanue family saw the arrival of Puerto Ricans as a business opportunity.

Goya Foods built a packing plant in Puerto Rico. They sold Puerto Rican foods there. They also exported them to the United States. Joseph Unanue said, "We had the products that reminded [people] of home."

Goya Foods moved into the Puerto Rican market by selling to bodegas. Bodegas are small local grocery stores. Goya salesmen supplied the shops with many foods. Salesmen visited stores daily. They wanted to learn what new foods customers wanted. The bodegas and Goya Foods developed strong ties over the years.

Goya Foods tried to place some of its products in larger supermarkets. At first, store owners refused to stock Goya's products. They didn't know what Spanish, Mexican, and Hispanic foods were. Many large stores didn't want to market to Hispanic customers. The first supermarket chain to stock Goya Foods was Safeway in Harlem, New York. Other supermarkets began to realize a growing demand for foods that Goya sold. They began offering Goya products, too.

In 1956, Unanue married Carmen Ana Casal. The couple later had six children. Many of their children (and grandchildren) would also work in Goya Foods when they grew up.

Over the next 25 years, Joseph Unanue worked in every area of the company. He worked in purchasing. He worked in production and distribution. He also worked in payroll, credit, and personnel. He even drove delivery trucks. He knew the job of every department. His engineering degree paid off, too, as the company began to expand and build new facilities.

In the late 1950s and early 1960s, there was a political change in Cuba. Fidel Castro took over in 1959. He was a dictator. Many Cubans who opposed Fidel Castro's new government left for America. Once again, Goya Foods responded to a new group of immigrants. They offered products that reminded Cubans of foods from home.

In the 1960s and 1970s, a new wave of immigrants from the Dominican Republic began arriving in New York. Goya Foods saw a new opportunity. They learned about Domincan foods. Goya added these products to their line. They targeted sales to Domincan communities.

Puerto Rican, Dominican, and Cuban foods have much in common. Each culture cooks with olive oil, garlic, and oregano. Some of the same items may be called different names by each community. In these cases, Goya Foods prints different labels for different neighborhoods. Joseph Unanue said, "If the Puerto Ricans call their beans *habichuelas,* we print the labels that go to Puerto Rican neighborhoods that way. We want to make sure shoppers find us right away."

Joseph Unanue became secretary and treasurer of Goya. His father, Prudencio, was president. But Prudencio became sick. Joseph took over as acting president. This means he did all the work of the president. But Joseph refused to be called president while his father was still alive. When Prudencio died in 1976, Joseph Unanue was named president of the company. He began an ambitious plan to reach the rest of the Latino community.

In the 1980s, Goya added foods enjoyed by even more Spanish-speaking cultures. They included foods cooked by Nicaraguans, Hondurans, Colombians, and other Central American people. In the 1990s, Goya offered products that appealed to South Americans from Peru, Ecuador, and Argentina.

Joseph Unanue explained his marketing strategy. He said, "Follow the trend of immigrating Hispanics who are coming in. Market the products people know from home."

Goya Foods turned its attention to Mexican Americans. They are the largest Hispanic community in the United States. This market was the most challenging for Goya. These shoppers were already loyal to brand names from Mexico.

To break into the market, Goya formed partnerships with Mexican food companies. Today Goya offers more than 75 Mexican products. Goya's name is gaining recognition among Mexican Americans.

The Hispanic market is complex. It includes people from about two dozen countries. While some foods are similar, each country has its own preferences. For example, different cultures often prefer different types of starchy foods. Mexicans cooks tend to prefer ingredients made from corn. Most South Americans cook with potatoes. Caribbean Hispanics and coastal South Americans prefer to cook with rice.

Goya makes sure each local store has the products its customers like. It does this by personally supplying each store. Other food companies use large distributors to deliver their products.

Goya Foods' top sellers include a variety of rice and more than 30 kinds of beans. Goya also sells oils, canned meats, flours, cookies and snacks, condiments, frozen foods, salsas, olives, beverages, pastas, and much more. A shopper could fill a cart with nothing but Goya products.

Goya Foods wants to attract non-Hispanic customers, too. Joseph Unanue said, "Just the way Italian food is now, one day Spanish food will be American food. Before (my father) died, he dreamed of the time when his company would not only become a well-known name in Latino homes, but also would be known to other segments of the American population."

The story of Goya Foods mirrors the history of Hispanics in America. As each new group of immigrants arrived, Goya Foods was there to meet their needs. Hispanic Americans have become part of mainstream America. In the same way, Goya Foods products are now used in homes across the country.

Goya Foods has also been a strong supporter of the cultural life of Latino communities. It has sponsored events that promote Hispanic cultural life. These include music events, sports teams, parades, beauty contests, and festivals.

Joseph Unanue and Goya Foods have had a long tradition of community service. The company supports many social, athletic, religious, and educational organizations.

In 2004, Joseph Unanue stepped down as president of Goya Foods. Robert Unanue, his nephew, took over. Joseph has remained on the board at Goya Foods, sharing his wealth of experience.

Joseph Unuane has continued to give back to the community. He and his wife donated $3 million to Seton Hall University. This money established the Joseph A. Unanue Latino Institute. The Institute offers Latino programs, including a major in Latino studies. At Catholic University of America, a campus dorm is named in honor of Unanue.

Joseph Unanue has received several honorary doctorate degrees from different colleges. He has earned countless awards for his community service. He was awarded the Ellis Island Medal of Honor. He has been named Man of the Year twice by the National Conference of Christians and Jews. He has received the Key to the City of Boston. He received the 1991 National Hispanic Achievement Award.

Joseph Unanue has given back to his community in many ways. He fought bravely in World War II. He worked hard to earn an education. He helped build his family business into a well-known national company. He made immigrants from Hispanic countries feel more at home. Joseph Unanue has used his success to help others. He has made a difference in the lives of Americans.

Remembering the Facts

1. Why did Prudencio Unanue begin importing foods from Spain?

2. Why did Prudencio Unanue buy the rights to the name "Goya" for his company?

3. Where were Goya's Puerto Rican foods first sold?

4. Which two groups of Hispanics began arriving in the United States in the 1960s?

5. Why was it hard for Goya Foods to break into the Mexican food market?

6. How does Goya Foods make sure local stores have the foods their customers like?

7. How does Goya Foods support the cultural life of Hispanic communities?

8. What is the purpose of the Joseph A. Unanue Latino Institute?

Understanding the Story

9.   Why is marketing to Hispanic Americans a complex undertaking?

10.   How has the story of Goya Foods paralleled the story of Hispanics in the United States?

Getting the Main Idea

In what ways do you think Joseph Unanue is a good role model for young Americans?

Applying What You've Learned

Find a Spanish, Mexican, or Hispanic recipe on the Internet or in a cookbook. Where is your dish from? Make a list of the ingredients your recipe requires.

Guy Gabaldon
U.S. Marine

Guy Gabaldon was a U.S. Marine private during World War II. At the time, the United States was at war with Japan. Using his courage and some Japanese phrases, Gabaldon captured 1,500 Japanese in the Battle of Saipan. Gabaldon was only 18 years old at the time.

During the battle, Japanese soldiers made suicide charges against the Americans. Entire families jumped off cliffs to avoid capture by the Americans. Private Gabaldon talked 1,500 Japanese people into peaceful surrender. He promised them they would be treated well. He said they would be given food and medical care.

For his bravery, Gabaldon was awarded the Navy Cross. It read, "Working alone in front of the lines, he daringly entered enemy caves, pillboxes, buildings, and jungle brush, frequently in the face of hostile fire, and succeeded in not only obtaining vital military information, but in capturing well over 1,000 enemy civilians and troops."

Guy Gabaldon was born on March 22, 1926, in Los Angeles, California. Guy was one of seven children. His father was a mechanic.

The Gabaldon family was Mexican American. They lived in the diverse community of Boyle Heights in East Los Angeles.

Guy was a member of the Moe Gang. This was not a gang as we think of gangs today. They were just boys sharing adventures. Seven of the boys were Japanese. Two were Mexican American. One was Jewish.

Guy was known for being fearless even then. Once, he jumped out of a second-story window on a dare. Another time, he hitched a ride on a freight train going to Barstow, California.

Guy had many jobs to earn money. At the age of ten, he shined shoes. He delivered Japanese newspapers. He also picked crops alongside his Japanese-American friends.

Two of Guy's friends in the Moe Gang were twins Lyle and Lane Nakano. Guy moved in with the Nakano family when he was 12 years old. Lyle and Lane taught Guy to speak some Japanese. Guy also went to language school with the twins. He learned much about Japanese customs.

Guy's world was turned upside down when he was 15 years old. Japan attacked Pearl Harbor, Hawaii, on December 7, 1941. The attack created much fear. The U.S. government arrested 100,000 people simply for being of Japanese descent. Many of these people were U.S. citizens who had been born in the United States.

The government put these people in internment camps. These camps contained structures that people lived in. Each camp was surrounded by barbed wire and armed guards. The purpose of internment camps is to confine a group of people who are selected for a specific reason. The U.S. government worried that Japanese Americans could be spies.

The Nakano family was sent to a camp in Arizona. They had no connection to the war. It was terrible for them and for Guy. The boys didn't get to say goodbye. Guy was left behind without his friends and extended family. He moved to Alaska to work in a cannery.

In 1943, the United States had been fighting in World War II for more than a year. Guy was now old enough to enlist in the military. He worried that the war would be over before he had a chance to fight for his country.

On his 17th birthday, Guy joined the Marines. After basic training, he was assigned to the 2nd Marine Regiment, 2nd Marine Division. He was a scout observer and an interpreter.

In 1943, the U.S. military planned an air attack on Japan. They planned to use a new American bomber called the B-29. It had a range of 2,850 miles. A group of islands called the Marianas were the right distance from Japan. The Americans would need to build air bases on the Mariana islands of Saipan, Tinian, and Guam to make the plan work. The only problem was that these islands were held by the Japanese. Many Japanese civilian families also lived on the islands.

The takeover of Saipan began on June 15, 1944. More than 500 U.S. ships arrived at the island. They were carrying 127,570 U.S. troops. Two-thirds of these were U.S. Marines from the 2nd and 4th divisions. Guy Gabaldon was one of them.

Seven U.S. battleships and eleven destroyers shelled the tiny islands of Saipan and Tinian for two days. They fired an enormous number of huge shells. This included 15,000 16-inch and 5-inch shells. (A 16-inch shell weighs more than a small car.)

On the second day of the battle, eight more battleships, six heavy cruisers, and five light cruisers joined the battle. Warships and bombers attacked the islands from all sides.

The Japanese did not surrender. They hid in caves and in the jungle. Ground troops would have to go in to force them out.

The main invasion force landed on Saipan along four miles of beach on June 15, 1944. Japanese shell fire rained down on the American troops. By the evening of the first day, 2,000 troops from the 2nd Marine Division had been killed, wounded, or captured. The fighting continued for nearly a month.

On his first night on the island, Guy Gabaldon went out on his own. He hoped that by working alone at night, he would be able to do something that no one else could.

That first night, he brought back two Japanese prisoners. For acting on his own, he was nearly put in the brig (military jail). He had left his post without permission. For this, Gabaldon received a reprimand by his superior officer, Capt. John Schwabe. (A reprimand is a formal military scolding for a wrong doing.) Luckily, Gabaldon did not have to face a court martial (military trial).

The next night, Gabaldon went out on his own again. He approached a cave where some Japanese were hiding. He shot the guards outside. Then he moved to the side of the cave. He thought of the Japanese words he had learned from his friends. In Japanese he shouted, "You're surrounded. You have no choice but to surrender. Come out, and you will not be killed. I assure you that you will be well treated. We do not want to kill you."

Gabaldon promised the Japanese that they would get food and medical care. He told them they would be taken back to Japan at the end of the war. He later said, "It had to be some kind of insanity to think that I could 'surround' them by myself. I really had no idea what kind of response I would get. When I began taking prisoners it became an addiction. I found that I couldn't stop. I was hooked. It became a way of life."

When Gabaldon returned to the Marine camp that second night, he brought 50 Japanese prisoners with him. Schwabe was amazed at the bravery of the 5'3" 18-year-old Marine. Schwabe later said, "He would go up to the mouth of a cave and jabber, jabber, jabber. And pretty soon somebody would dribble out."

The prisoners Gabaldon brought in had useful information for the Marines. This information could save the lives of other soldiers. It might even end the Battle of Saipan sooner. So Gabaldon was allowed to continue his "lone-wolf" operations.

Gabaldon later said, "I must have seen too many John Wayne movies, because what I was doing was suicidal. It was foolish to believe that I would be the only Marine that could capture the enemy Japanese."

On the night of July 7, 1944, Gabaldon was near the northern cliffs of the island. He heard plans being made for a suicide attack. Gabaldon returned to camp with this information.

When the Japanese attacked, the Marines were ready for them. The attack lasted for 15 hours. But it was not successful. The surviving Japanese returned to their caves in the hills.

The next night, Gabaldon captured two Japanese guards. He talked one of them into returning to the cave to talk his friends into surrendering. He told them, "Why die when you have a chance to surrender under honorable conditions? You are taking civilians with you, which is not part of your military code." Soon a Japanese officer came to Gabaldon. He accepted the terms of surrender.

In the meantime, Marine patrols were moving up from the beach to map out the Japanese lines. As they approached the cliffs, they couldn't believe what they saw. One small American Marine was surrounded by hundreds of Japanese troops. Many of these troops were still armed.

As the scouts watched, more Japanese kept coming out from their hiding places. Then the scouts realized that the lone Marine was organizing the Japanese into groups. Gabaldon separated the military from civilians. He got all the wounded in one area to be taken for medical care.

More than 800 soldiers and civilians surrendered to Gabaldon. He returned to the Marine camp leading all 800. After that, Gabaldon was known as the Pied Piper of Saipan.

In all, the Battle of Saipan lasted 24 days. The suicides of hundreds of island families were devastating. Adults and children jumped to their deaths from the high cliffs. They jumped out of fear that the "American Savages" would roast and eat their children.

Guy Gabaldon tried to stop them. He shouted at them, begging them not to jump. But most jumped off the cliff and were killed. Gabaldon later said, "This was truly the horror of war."

Gabaldon continued his nightly missions until he was wounded by enemy machine-gun fire. He was sent to a hospital. Later he was given an honorable discharge from the Marines because of his wounds.

When the fighting ended on July 9, more than 46,000 Japanese and Americans had died. Of the U.S. troops, 3,100 had died. Another 13,100 were wounded or missing in action. Almost all of the 30,000 Japanese troops were dead, along with 22,000 civilians. About 2,100 prisoners survived. Most of these prisoners had been saved by Guy Gabaldon.

The official end to the fighting on Saipan was on July 9, 1944. Much of the combat had been hand-to-hand. Besides rifles and machine guns, battles were fought with swords, bamboo spears, clubs, and stones.

But the actual final surrender was not until nearly five months later. Japanese Army Captain Sakeo Oba had remained hidden in the mountains with his 46 men. Finally, on December 1, 1945, he surrendered his samurai sword.

The fighting in the Pacific continued for another 13 months. On August 6, 1945, the United States dropped the first atomic bomb on Hiroshima, Japan. Japan surrendered, ending World War II.

Gabaldon was given credit for the capture of 1,500 Japanese. Capt. Schwabe recommended him for the Medal of Honor, the military's highest award. Instead, he was given a Silver Star, an award just below the Medal of Honor.

After the war, Gabaldon moved to Mexico. There he had various businesses. These included a furniture store, being a skipper on a fishing boat, and exporting Mexican goods. He also met and married his second wife, Ohana Suzuki. (His first marriage had ended in divorce.)

In 1957, Gabaldon was featured on the television show *This Is Your Life*. This was a popular NBC show in the 1950s. The program told the life stories of various interesting people. People from the guest's past made appearances on the show. John Schwabe, now a colonel, was there to tell the story of Gabaldon's capture of 1,500 Japanese.

Movie producers saw the show. They thought Gabaldon's story would make a great movie. They asked Gabaldon to be an advisor on a movie about his adventures. In 1960, *Hell to Eternity* was released.

Gabaldon's feats were now widely known. On November 23, 1960, the government upgraded his Silver Star medal to the Navy Cross medal. This is the Marine Corps' second-highest medal.

In 1970, Gabaldon moved to Saipan with his wife. He ran a seafood business. He also wrote a book. *Saipan: Suicide Island* (1990) told the story of his wartime experience.

In 1995, Gabaldon moved back to California. Then in 2003, he moved to Florida. He died there on August 31, 2006. He was survived by his wife and eight children.

Gabaldon received many honors for his work. In 2004, he traveled to Saipan to speak at the 60th anniversary of the Battle of Saipan. He also spoke at the 2004 dedication of the World War II Memorial in Washington, D.C.

In 2006, military artist Henry Godines made a painting of Gabaldon. It is called "Pied Piper of Saipan, Guy Gabaldon."

After his death, many groups requested that Guy Gabaldon be awarded the Medal of Honor. Some feel that he was not given the medal because of his ethnic background.

A documentary film about his life, *East L.A. Marine: The Untold True Story of Guy Gabaldon*, was released in 2006. In the film, Gabaldon explained his courage. "Being raised in the barrio, every day is a fight. You're fighting to survive in the barrio, and I think that might have had something to do with my makeup."

Guy Gabaldon has become a folk hero. He was an outstanding Marine and a tough fighter. At the same time, he treated his enemies with compassion. He treated them as fellow human beings. That is the greatness of Guy Gabaldon.

Remembering the Facts

1. How did Guy learn Japanese when he was young?

2. Why was the Moe Gang broken up in 1941?

3. Why was the U.S. military determined to capture the tiny island of Saipan?

4. Why were ships and bombers unable to force the surrender of Saipan?

5. How did Gabaldon convince the Japanese to surrender to him?

6. Why was Gabaldon allowed to continue his "lone-wolf" operation?

7. Why did many Japanese families commit suicide by jumping off the cliffs?

8. What movie about Gabaldon's story was released in 1960?

Understanding the Story

9. How do you think Gabaldon's experiences growing up in the Moe Gang helped him accomplish what he did as a Marine?

10. Why do you think Gabaldon's war actions attracted the attention of movie makers and artists?

Getting the Main Idea

In what ways is Guy Gabaldon's story an important part of American history?

Applying What You've Learned

Write a paragraph explaining what you think 18-year-old Gabaldon might have felt as he waited outside a cave full of Japanese soldiers, hoping they would surrender.

Nicholasa Mohr
Artist/Writer

Nicholasa Mohr writes novels and short stories, mostly for teens and younger readers. She is also the illustrator for many of her books.

Mohr writes about life in the Puerto Rican slums of New York City. She says, "(My work makes) a strong social statement. (It talks about) the constant struggle of the Puerto Ricans on the mainland to receive their basic human rights."

Nicholasa Golpe Mohr was born on November 1, 1938, in New York City. She was the youngest of seven children. She had six older brothers.

Nicholasa's mother, Nicholasa Rivera, had moved to New York City from Puerto Rico. It was during the Great Depression in the 1930s. She was a 22-year-old single mother with four small sons. In New York, she met Pedro Golpe. He was a merchant seaman from Spain. The couple married. They had three more children, including Nicholasa.

The family lived in a New York neighborhood known as Spanish Harlem. It was called Spanish Harlem because so many people living there spoke Spanish. One part of Spanish Harlem was called El Barrio. This was a particularly poor area. The Golpes lived there. Later, the family moved to the Bronx. This was another section of New York City.

Nicholasa grew up bilingual. She and her brothers spoke English outside their home. Their parents always spoke Spanish.

Her family believed in strict roles for males and females. As the only girl, Nicholasa had to help with the housework. Her brothers had the freedom to go out with their friends. Nicholasa was seldom allowed to go out. She spent most of her free time at home.

The Golpe family loved stories. Mohr later said, "Storytelling has always been an important part of Puerto Rican culture. When our family faced difficulties, an adult would say, 'Don't lose hope, sit back and relax, and I'll tell you a story.' ... Our problems and burdens began to seem lighter, and life appeared promising."

Nicholasa's brothers taught her to read before she started first grade. She got her first library card when she was seven years old. The library became a second home for her. She later said, "My access to the New York Public Library was what allowed me to pursue my thirst for knowledge. It was there that I sought out an education for myself."

School was hard for Nicholasa. She said that it was like "entering into hostile territory." Teachers and classmates looked down on the Puerto Rican students. One day, Nicholasa tried to help some new students who didn't speak English. She spoke to them in Spanish. The teacher yelled, "This is not your country! You speak English here!"

When Nicholasa was eight, her father died. Her father had taught her many important lessons. She later said, "Like him, I think that people must work hard and respect each other on this planet. Good deeds and faith in our fellow human beings are necessary for our survival."

Nicholasa grieved for her father. Her mother gave her paper, a pencil, and some crayons to help her work out her grief.

Nicholasa later said, "From the moment my mother handed me some scrap paper, a pencil, and a few crayons, I discovered that by making pictures and writing letters I could create my own world, like 'magic.' In the small, crowded apartment I shared with my large family, making 'magic' permitted me all the space, freedom, and adventure that my imagination could handle. Drawing and painting were my first loves. Later, I began to write and to paint pictures with words."

Nicholasa's mother struggled to support her family. She was determined to take care of them. She worked in small sewing "sweatshop." A sweatshop is a shop or factory with very poor working conditions and low pay. For her hard work, Nicholasa's mother received little pay.

Nicholasa's mother encouraged her artwork. She said, "You must always do your work and respect the wonderful gift God has given you." It was understood that Nicholasa would go to college to study art.

Nicholasa's mother became ill with cancer. Before she died, she made Nicholasa promise that she would find a way to become an artist no matter what happened.

Nicholasa was 14 when her mother died. She went to live with her aunt. Her aunt didn't want to be bothered with another child to raise. She was very cold toward Nicholasa. Nicholasa comforted herself with her drawing.

Just before her mother's death, Nicholasa had finished middle school. She was an excellent student. Some teachers at her school did not treat Nicholasa well because she was Puerto Rican. In fact, one middle school counselor nearly ended Nicholasa's education.

Nicholasa wanted to attend the High School of Music & Art. A counselor signed her up for a trade school instead. She had decided that Nicholasa should become a seamstress. The counselor didn't encourage Puerto Rican girls to earn an academic education.

Nicholasa said, "I remember pleading with her to let me at least apply to a better high school. She answered that Puerto Rican women were by nature good seamstresses. Therefore, I should follow a natural career and be able to earn a living after graduation."

Nicholasa went to Stabermore High School, a trade school. Luckily the school offered a major in fashion illustration. Nicholasa had no interest in this kind of art. But at least she was able to draw instead of operating a sewing machine.

After graduating from high school, Nicholasa attended The Arts Students League in New York City. She worked her way through school. She earned enough to pay her expenses. She attended this school from 1953 to 1956.

Nicholasa had studied the work of many famous Mexican artists. She loved the work of Diego Rivera, Frida Kahlo, and José Clemente Orozco. Nicholasa saved her money. She eventually had enough to travel to Mexico City to attend the Taller de Gráfica printmaking workshop. There she could study the works she loved firsthand.

The powerful work of these Mexican artists thrilled Nicholasa. She saw how their work made strong statements about issues important to them. She later said, "In a profound way, their work spoke to me and my experiences as a Puerto Rican woman born in New York. The impact was to shape and form the direction of all my future work."

When she returned to New York, she enrolled in the New School for Social Research. There she met her future husband, Irwin Mohr. They married in 1957. The couple later had two children, David and Jason.

Nicholasa Mohr worked to develop her own unique style. Her art often told a story. She hoped that her art would invoke feelings in the viewer. She said, "My prints and paintings were filled with bold figures, faces, and various symbols of the city. These symbols were numbers, letters, words, and phrases . . . a kind of graffiti." By the late 1960s, Mohr was a recognized painter in the New York art world.

A publishing company executive loved Mohr's artwork. He understood how her work told stories. He thought she might be good at writing stories using words rather than paint.

At first, Mohr was not interested. Her agent talked her into it. The agent told Mohr that her work would fill a gap in children's literature. There were no stories about young Puerto Ricans at that time.

Mohr realized that was true. She said, "When I was growing up, I'd enjoyed reading about the adventures of many boys and girls. But I had never really seen myself, my brothers, and my family in those books. We were just not there."

Mohr wrote several short stories. She based her stories on her childhood growing up in the barrio. The publisher didn't like her stories. Her publisher was looking for stories of drama. Mohr's stories were about her life. They were not about gangs, sex, or drugs. So the publisher didn't think they were realistic.

Mohr said, "I knew then that I did not exist for him as the person I really was. I was just a model for a Puerto Rican (heroine) who would be featured in a sensational book that he (thought) would make us a fortune."

Mohr thought that was the end of her writing career. She went back to her drawing board.

Soon, another publishing company called her. The editor, Ellen Rudin, wanted Mohr to do some book illustrations. When she learned that Mohr had written some stories, she offered to look them over.

Rudin thought Mohr had writing talent. She offered her a contract to write a novel for young adults. Mohr's first book, *Nilda*, was published in 1973. Mohr also created eight illustrations and the cover art. Mohr dedicated the book to the children of the barrio.

Nilda is the story of a young Puerto Rican girl growing up in El Barrio during World War II. Nilda faces poverty and prejudice. She finds that writing stories and drawing pictures helps her deal with these problems.

Mohr said that she realized that "I could draw a picture with words. It was extremely stimulating and eye opening. Everything I (had) done as an artist (was) transferable to a new craft." Mohr also said that writing can be enjoyed by more people than artwork.

Nilda won many awards for juvenile fiction. Mohr was the first woman to write in English about the lives of Puerto Ricans in New York.

Mohr went on to write many more books. Her second book, *El Bronx Remembered* (1975), takes place in Nilda's neighborhood after the end of the war. The stories tell of serious issues in the neighborhood. They are also stories of optimism and hope.

In 1978, Mohr's husband died. She moved from New Jersey to Brooklyn. Once again, she worked out her grief through her writing.

Mohr wrote two novels about a Puerto Rican girl named Felita. *Felita* (1979) and *Going Home* (1986) are written for younger readers. Felita's family moves away from the barrio to a better neighborhood. But Felita misses her old neighborhood. The new neighbors don't want Puerto Ricans living there. In the end, the family moves back to face the old familiar problems in the old neighborhood.

Mohr published a book of folktales in 1995. *The Song of El Coqui and Other Tales of Puerto Rico* includes three folktales. Each tale tells about a part of the culture of Puerto Rico.

In 1999, Mohr created a musical adaptation of her novel *Nilda*. She has adapted many of her other works as screenplays, dramas, and teleplays. Today she continues to adapt her works for the stage.

In 2001, Mohr moved back to the neighborhood where she grew up. She has a loft in East Harlem, El Barrio. There she continues her writing. She finds her work very rewarding. She said, "As a writer I have used my abilities as a creative artist to strengthen my skills and at the same time (be) a voice for my ethnic American community and our children."

Mohr's work reaches children of all backgrounds. She says, "My books are very Latino, but they're not written for Latinos. I write from the heart about what I know and feel strongly about."

Mohr continued, "I feel blessed by the work I do, for it permits me to use my talents and continue to 'make magic.' With this 'magic' I can recreate those deepest of personal memories as well as … celebrate my heritage and my future."

Mohr often speaks at colleges. She has been a visiting professor at several universities. She encourages young Hispanics to become writers. She says, "I hope there will be more Hispanic writers finding their voices too, learning to value their own lives as important and valuable to write about."

Nicholasa Mohr has received many honors and awards. In 2003, she won the Women of El Barrio Woman of Substance Award. In 2006, she received the NYS Hispanic Heritage Month Award. In June 2007, the Puerto Rican Family Institute awarded her the Raul Julia Award.

In 1989, Nicholasa Mohr received an honorary doctorate from the State University of New York. The citation read (in part): "You, Nicholasa Mohr, have captured in your fiction an essential part of the diverse culture of this country. Your work paints a poignant picture of the Puerto Rican experience that has touched the hearts of all readers. You serve as witness and translator of the joys and sorrows … of this immigrant group that, together with many others, has contributed to the character of this country. You have enriched our understanding of our nation and the struggles of its diverse peoples."

Remembering the Facts

1. What is the topic of most of Mohr's writing?

2. What function has storytelling served in Puerto Rican families?

3. How did Nicholasa work out her grief after her father died?

4. How did a guidance counselor almost end Nicholasa's chances for success?

5. Why did Nicholasa go to Mexico City?

6. Describe Mohr's style as an artist in the 1960s.

7. What is the book *Nilda* about?

8. Why did Mohr's work fill an important niche in children's literature?

Understanding the Story

9. Explain how Nicholasa overcame the many challenges she faced as a young Puerto Rican girl in the barrio.

10. In what ways do you think drawing a picture and writing a story could be similar?

Getting the Main Idea

In what ways do you think Nicholasa Mohr is a good role model for young Americans?

Applying What You've Learned

Write a brief story about a young person growing up in your own neighborhood. If you prefer, you could draw a picture on the same subject.

Isabel Allende
Author

Isabel Allende is one of the best-selling Hispanic-American woman novelists. She writes in the style of "magical realism." This style is common in Latin American literature. It weaves real and imaginary events together to form a story. Allende has received awards from around the world for her writing.

Isabel Allende was born on August 2, 1942, in Lima, Peru. Her father, Tomás Allende, was secretary of the Chilean Embassy in Peru. Her mother, Francisca, stayed at home. Isabel had two younger brothers. All three children were born in Peru, even though their parents were from Chile. The family had moved to Peru for Tomás's job.

When Isabel was three years old, her parents separated. Francisca took her children back to live with her family in Santiago, Chile. Isabel never spoke to her father again. The family never spoke of him.

The children grew up in their grandfather's house. Her mother and two uncles also lived there. Isabel's grandfather was Agustín Cuevas. He was a successful businessman. His house was large. Many servants took care of the family's needs. Isabel's grandfather taught her to work hard. He told her that the highest goal is success.

Isabel's grandmother was often ill. She walked the halls of the huge house in a daze. She claimed to have magical powers. She said she could predict the future. When Isabel's grandmother felt well, she worked to help poor people in the slums of Santiago.

Isabel was young when her grandmother died. Her family mourned the loss. Her grandfather had all the furniture in the house painted black. Everyone in the house had to dress in black. The large house became a dark, frightening place. Isabel imagined evil spirits haunting the hallways.

Isabel found a way to escape her sadness. Her Uncle Pablo shared many books with her. Isabel spent hours reading. She loved to escape into a good adventure or detective story. She liked to play make-believe games in the large basement of the house. Isabel developed a very good imagination.

One day Isabel found a trunk in the basement. It was full of books that had belonged to her father. At last Isabel had something that had belonged to her father. Isabel read the books. But no one would ever answer her questions about her father.

Isabel's mother, Francisca, worked at a local bank to help support her family. At night, she told her children many old family stories. Isabel learned to love storytelling, too.

On Sundays, the family would often hike to the top of a hill in the center of town. There they would picnic and play games. Often they were joined by Tomás's cousin, Salvador Allende. He was a politician in Chile.

When Isabel was ten, her mother remarried. Her new husband was a diplomat named Ramón Huidobro. Isabel called him "Tío Ramón," which means "Uncle Ramón." The family moved to La Paz, Bolivia.

Isabel was very sad to leave her grandfather. She felt as though her childhood had ended. Isabel's mother gave her a journal. In it, she wrote about her feelings and new experiences. From that day on, Isabel has always kept a journal. She says the journal helps her "sort out the confusion of life."

The family was not in La Paz for long. When Isabel was 12, Tío Ramón was sent to work in Beirut, Lebanon. This is a country in the Middle East. The family went with him.

Isabel went to an English private girls' school in Beirut. No one at the school had heard of Chile. They all thought Isabel was Chinese.

At the school, she learned to speak English and French. She memorized Bible verses. Discipline was strict. The food was awful. The girls ate unsalted rice with vegetables or liver every day. Yet, Isabel felt safe and comfortable in the school's predictable setting.

In 1958, fighting broke out in Beirut. Life became very dangerous. Isabel's family put mattresses in front of the windows to keep stray bullets out of their apartment. Finally, Tío Ramón sent the children back to Chile to live with their grandfather again. Tío Ramón and Francisca stayed in Beirut. Isabel wrote a letter to her mother every day.

Back in Chile, Isabel enrolled in school. Because the family had moved so much, she was behind in several subjects. Her grandfather hired a math tutor for her. He tutored her in history and geography himself. Isabel and her grandfather became very close.

The two loved each other, but they didn't see eye to eye. Her grandfather believed strongly in "machismo." Machismo is the idea that women and men are not equal. Isabel's grandfather thought that women were helpless and needed men to take care of them. Most men in Chile in those days had the same belief.

Isabel was already a feminist. She believed that men and women should be treated equally. In the 1950s, this was a radical way to think. Isabel and her grandfather had many heated arguments on the subject. Later, the theme of feminism would be an important part of Isabel's writing.

In 1959, Isabel received her high-school diploma. She got a job with a United Nations agency. It was the Food and Agriculture Organization (FAO).

She got a second job translating romance novels from English to Spanish. Allende thought the women in the novels she read were silly.

So she re-wrote some of the things they said and did. She often changed the endings of the books. She wanted the women to be strong and do good deeds. Allende was soon fired from that job.

In 1962, Isabel Allende married Miguel Frías. He was an engineering student. The couple later had two children, Paula and Nicholás. Allende managed to have both a career and a family life as a wife and mother.

As part of her job for the FAO, Allende was asked to go on TV. She was to explain a U.N. program called the World Campaign Against Hunger. She did a good job. The station asked her to do a weekly TV program.

In 1967, Allende began writing for a women's magazine called *Paula*. She was to do a weekly humorous column. In her column, Allende focused on women's issues. She wrote about divorce, birth control, and women's rights. Her work was daring in a society that thought women had few rights. Allende worked for *Paula* for the next seven years.

From 1970 to 1975, Allende was on two popular TV shows. One was an interview program. The other show dealt with serious issues in a light-hearted way.

In September 1970, Isabel's cousin Salvador Allende was elected president of Chile. Salvador Allende was a socialist. Some people did not like his policies. They were afraid he would ruin Chile's economy. In September 1973, the Chilean military took over the government by force. Salvador Allende was killed.

Life in Chile became very dangerous for anyone who had supported Salvador Allende. Many people were thrown in jail. Many more just disappeared and were never heard from again.

Over the next 18 months, Isabel Allende helped people who were trying to hide from the new government. She gave them food. She let them stay in her home. This work put her and her family in grave danger. Finally, they had to flee the country in 1975. They went to Caracas, Venezuela. They stayed there for 13 years.

Allende was unable to find work as a writer in Venezuela. She became a school manager in 1979. She worked at the school for 12 hours a day for the next four years.

In 1981, Allende learned that her grandfather was very ill. She was sad she could not return to Chile to be with him. If she did, she could be thrown in jail or even killed.

Allende began writing her grandfather a letter. In it she told him many family stories. She worked on the letter every night after work. It became longer and longer. Finally, she had written 500 pages. The letter became her first novel, *The House of the Spirits*. It was published in 1982.

The book contained many real events in Allende's life. It told real family stories. It told of the military coup in Chile. But it also wove in imaginary events with these true events. Allende tells these strange events as if they really happened.

The book was a huge success. It was named best novel of the year 1982 in Chile. It was published in the United States in 1985. It quickly became successful there, too. It was made into a movie in 1993.

Allende's second novel, *Of Love and Shadows*, was published in 1984. It tells the story of women whose husbands or sons disappeared after the military takeover in Chile. It tells of a country struggling to survive under military rule. Yet it shows the love and caring people have for each other in the most trying times.

In 1987, Allende and her husband divorced after 25 years of marriage. The next year, she met an American lawyer named William Gordon. He had read *Of Love and Shadows*. He came to a lecture she was giving in San Jose, California, hoping to meet her.

The two were married in 1988. They moved to San Rafael, California. Allende began teaching creative writing at the University of California at Berkeley. She became an American citizen.

In 1990, democracy was established in Chile once again. For the first time in 15 years, Allende could return to her native land. While there, she received the Gabriela Mistral Award. This award was given in memory of Gabriela Mistral. She was a writer who won the Nobel Prize in Literature in 1945.

Allende's daughter Paula became very ill on December 6, 1991. By the time Allende arrived at the hospital, Paula had gone into a coma.

Allende sat by Paula's bedside for many months. As she sat, she told the story of their family to Paula. She told Paula her childhood memories. She spun story after story about various colorful ancestors. She passed along many family secrets to her unconscious daughter. Allende also wrote down her stories.

Paula died one year to the day after she had become sick. Allende began making the stories she had written at Paula's bedside into a book. *Paula* was published in 1994. This memoir is thought by many to be Allende's finest work.

Allende decided she would use the money she made from sales of the novel *Paula* to help others. Paula had spent much time working as a volunteer in poor villages in Venezuela and Spain. Her motto had been, "When in doubt, what is the most generous thing to do?"

Allende set up the Isabel Allende Foundation in 1996. Its purpose was to continue Paula's work. The foundation supports groups in San Francisco and Chile that help women and children. It provides funds for education, health care, and other needs.

Allende's first book set in the United States was *The Infinite Plan.* This book, published in 1993, is based on the life of her husband, William Gordon.

Allende continued her writing. *Aphrodite: A Memoir of the Senses* was published in 1997. It combined a cookbook and a memoir.

Daughter of Fortune was published in 1999. It is the story of a young girl's adventures during the California Gold Rush. Oprah Winfrey liked the book. She picked it for her book club. This was the first time Oprah had picked a book written by a Hispanic author. Oprah also interviewed Allende on *The Oprah Winfrey Show*. Sales of the book soared. Allende became one of the best-selling female authors in the world.

Allende has received many awards and honors. In 1998, she received the Dorothy and Lillian Gish Prize. This prize is given to a person "who has contributed to the beauty of the world … and to our enjoyment and understanding of life." She has also received a number of honorary doctorates.

In 2000, Allende published *Portrait in Sepia*. This book featured some of the same characters from *The House of the Spirits* and *Daughter of Fortune*. Together, the three books form a trilogy. In 2003, Allende published *My Invented Country*.

Isabel Allende's grandchildren asked her to write a story for them. So she wrote a children's trilogy. It included *City of the Beasts* (2002), *Kingdom of the Golden Dragon* (2003), and *Forest of the Pygmies* (2005).

In 2008, Allende published *The Sum of Our Days*. This book picks up the story of Allende's life where *Paula* leaves off.

Allende has loved to write all her life. She once said, "I write to communicate, to survive, to make the world more understandable. I write because if I didn't I would die." On her Web site, Allende says, "Nothing makes my soul sing more than writing. It makes me feel young, strong, powerful, happy. Wow!"

She continues, "My most significant achievements are not my books, but the love I share with a few people, especially my family, and the ways in which I have tried to help others. When I was young, I often felt desperate. So much pain in the world and so little I could do to alleviate it! But now I look back at my life and feel satisfied because few days went by without at least trying."

Remembering the Facts

1. What is magical realism?

2. When did Isabel learn to love reading?

3. How did Isabel's mother give her a love of storytelling?

4. What did Isabel often argue with her grandfather about?

5. Why were Allende and her family forced to flee Chile in 1975?

6. How did her grandfather's illness cause Allende to write her first book?

7. Why did Allende write the book *Paula*?

8. What is the purpose of the Isabel Allende Foundation?

Understanding the Story

9. Isabel Allende has said, "I write to communicate, to survive, to make the world more understandable. I write because if I didn't I would die."

   What do you think Allende means by this statement?

10. How do you think the Isabel Allende Foundation works toward Allende's feminist ideals?

Getting the Main Idea

In what ways do you think Isabel Allende is a good role model for young Americans?

Applying What You've Learned

Write about an event in your life using the style of magical realism. The event itself should be real. But along with the facts in your account, put in imaginary details.

Mario Molina
Scientist

On December 10, 1995, Mario Molina stood in front of the king and queen of Sweden. He was one of three scientists who had won the Nobel Prize in Chemistry. They had made the alarming discovery that chlorofluorocarbons (CFCs) were destroying part of the earth's ozone layer.

The presenter of the award said, "You have contributed to our salvation from a global environmental problem that could have had catastrophic consequences.... In the words of Alfred Nobel's will, your work has been of very great benefit to mankind." Mario Molina was the first Mexican American to win the Nobel Prize.

Mario Molina was born in Mexico City, Mexico, on March 19, 1943. He was the fourth of seven children. Mario's father, Roberto Molina Pasquel, was a lawyer. His father also taught at the Universidad Nacional Autónoma de México (UNAM). (This is the National University of Mexico.)

When Mario was a boy, Mexico City had no air pollution. From his home, he could see two mountains topped with snow. Mario loved the old Aztec story of the two mountains, Iztaccihuatl and Popocatepetl.

Iztaccihuatl was a princess. She was in love with Popocatepetl. He was one of her father's warriors. The king did not want her to marry a warrior. So he sent the young man to fight in a war far away. He said that if the warrior returned, he could marry the princess. The king told the princess that her love had died. She died of grief. But the warrior returned alive. He died of grief from losing her. So the Aztec gods turned them both into mountains to be forever side by side.

The mountain Iztaccihuatl is a volcano. It has been extinct for 80,000 years. But Popocatepetl is one of the most active volcanoes in Mexico. It erupted in 2000. Thousands of people had to be evacuated. People say Popocatepetl is the warrior still raining fire on the earth in his grief.

Mexico City's businesses were growing when Mario was a child. Cars and industry created pollution. As Mario grew older, the air quality in Mexico City became worse. The two towering mountains could rarely be seen. Mario didn't know it then, but the study of air pollution would later become his life's work.

As a child, Mario took violin lessons. He was very talented. His parents were pleased. They thought he would become a concert violinist.

The violin did not hold his interest for long. When he was a child, Mario was given a toy microscope. He began playing with it. He put a drop of water under the microscope. He looked and saw tiny things swimming about. Mario was thrilled with the new world he had found.

Mario's aunt, Esther Molina, was a chemist. She was glad to learn of Mario's interest in science. She guided him. She helped him plan experiments. Mario spent more and more time with his microscope.

Mario's parents let him make one of their bathrooms into a chemistry lab. Mario worked in his lab every day. Sometimes he studied chemicals he found in the house. He researched what they were made of. Other times he mixed substances. He formed new mixtures. His family never knew what strange smells might greet them when they entered the house.

Mario tried to get his friends to work in his lab. No one was interested. They thought science was boring. They preferred playing outside. Mario later said, "My studies in chemistry were a lonely adventure."

When Mario was 11, his parents sent him to a boarding school. It was in Switzerland. They thought it was important for him to study abroad. Mario hoped the students at his new school would like science. He soon found out they did not.

No one else at the school spoke Spanish. But there were several Italian students. Mario soon realized that Spanish and Italian had much in common. He learned to speak Italian easily. Since his classes were taught in German, he learned that, too.

Mario went to the boarding school for two years. He returned to Mexico City for high school. In 1960, he graduated from high school. He entered the Universidad Nacional Autónoma de México (UNAM). He majored in chemical engineering. He studied how to use chemistry in industry. He graduated in 1965.

Mario Molina decided to study how to use physics in chemical systems. First he needed to learn more math and physics. He studied at the University of Freiburg in Germany for two years. He earned a degree similar to a master's degree.

In 1968, Molina entered a program to become a doctor in physical chemistry. He studied to get his Ph.D. at the University of California at Berkeley. He knew little English, but he learned quickly. He also decided to become a U.S. citizen.

At Berkeley, he met a chemistry student named Luisa Tan. She had grown up in the Philippines. The two became friends. Molina offered to teach her to drive. The two were married in July 1973. They later had a son, Felipe.

Molina found the friends he had longed for at last. The students at Berkeley loved science just as he did. Molina found life stimulating and exciting.

In 1968, the United States was involved in the Vietnam War. The war was very unpopular with students around the country. Many anti-war protests were held on the Berkeley campus.

Molina was working with the research group that had discovered chemical lasers. Chemical lasers get their energy from chemical reactions. Molina's project was to use the lasers to see how molecules act during chemical reactions.

But scientists in other places were using chemical lasers to make weapons. So Molina's work was unpopular with students. Molina said, "I was dismayed that chemical lasers were being developed elsewhere as weapons. I wanted to be involved with research that was useful to society, not for harmful purposes."

Molina received his degree in 1972. He moved to Irvine, California. There, he did post-doctoral work with Dr. F. Sherwood Rowland. Molina hoped to do work that would benefit humanity.

Rowland and Molina were interested in the effects of chemicals released into the air. Two years earlier, a Dutch scientist, Paul Crutzen, had shown that chlorine could break down ozone molecules. Studies had also been done on the effects of chlorine from volcanic eruptions. The effect of chlorine from rocket-engine fuel had been studied. But no one had thought about the chlorine in chlorofluorocarbons (CFCs).

CFCs are a family of chemical compounds. They were developed back in the 1930s. They were thought to be safe cooling agents and spray-can propellants. They were widely used in refrigerators and air conditioners. Spray paint, hairspray, bug sprays, and many other products contained CFCs. Molina decided to study CFCs.

Molina wondered what happened to them when they entered the atmosphere. He said, "It seemed that maybe nothing whatsoever interesting would happen to them."

Molina knew that CFCs appeared to be harmless when released into the air. They just float about in their original form. But after two to five years, they are carried by winds high into the upper level of the atmosphere. This level is called the stratosphere.

Molina found that an alarming thing happened to CFCs in the stratosphere. The sun's rays break the CFC molecules down into atoms. One of these atoms is chlorine.

Chlorine atoms destroy a form of oxygen called ozone. Just one chlorine atom can destroy as many as 100,000 ozone molecules. Millions of tons of CFCs were being released every year. Molina and Rowland were alarmed. They knew that the destruction of the ozone layer could threaten life on Earth.

The ozone layer is found between 6 to 30 miles above the earth's surface. It absorbs the sun's ultraviolet (UV) rays. UV rays are harmful to both animals and plants. Too much UV radiation can cause skin cancer, eye damage, and other problems. It also affects the growth of many important crops.

Molina and Rowland published their findings in the June 28, 1974, issue of the journal *Nature*. They stated that CFCs could be destroying the ozone layer. Most people ignored the findings.

Scientists were critical of Molina's work. Industries that used CFCs were not happy. It would be costly for them to change their products.

Molina and Rowland began a public awareness campaign in 1975. They wrote magazine articles about CFCs. Their work was featured in news stories. They met with business and government leaders. People began writing their members of Congress about CFCs. Molina said, "Eventually we caught people's attention."

The U.S. government passed amendments to the Clean Air Act in 1977. They called for the regulation of any substance "reasonably anticipated to affect the stratosphere." The United States banned the use of CFCs as propellants in spray cans.

In 1985, Molina's theory was proven right. Scientists discovered a large hole in the ozone layer over Antarctica. During the winter, the hole was nearly the size of the continental United States. This discovery made news around the world. Something more had to be done.

In September 1987, more than two dozen countries signed the Montreal Protocol. The treaty called for CFCs to be phased out by 1995 in most countries.

Mario Molina continued his research on other chemicals that enter the atmosphere. He worked as a professor at the University of California at Irvine from 1975 to 1982. His wife worked with him on some of his projects.

Between 1982 and 1989, Molina worked at the California Institute of Technology. In 1989, he took a teaching position at the Massachusetts Institute of Technology (MIT).

Molina enjoyed teaching. He said, "I have always benefited from teaching. As I try to explain my views to students with critical and open minds, I find myself continually being challenged to go back and rethink those ideas."

One morning in 1995, Molina was preparing to teach a class at MIT. He got a call from the Royal Academy of Sciences in Stockholm, Sweden. The caller said that he had been awarded a Nobel Prize in Chemistry for his work with CFCs. He would share the $1 million prize with two other scientists. They were Paul Crutzen and F. Sherwood Rowland.

After winning the Nobel Prize, Molina was in demand as a speaker. He used his new fame. He gave talks about human activities that pollute the air. He continued his work studying air pollution.

Air pollution is a problem around the world. Molina wanted to encourage students to study atmospheric chemistry. So, in 1996, he donated nearly two-thirds of his Nobel Prize money to MIT. It was to be used to help international students come to the United States to study atmospheric science.

Molina's birthplace, Mexico City, had a severe air pollution problem. In 2000, Molina helped start a project to reduce the air pollution.

In 2002, he and his wife published a book titled *Air Quality in the Mexico Megacity*. This book included the ideas of many scientists on how to improve the air quality in Mexico City. Today, the air quality in Mexico City has greatly improved.

In 2005, Molina took a position at the University of California, San Diego. Also in 2005, Molina and his wife opened the Molina Center for Strategic Studies in Energy and the Environment. It is an independent non-profit organization that brings together international experts in science and engineering, economics, and social and political sciences. The group works together to research, advise, and train the public on issues. The center is in La Jolla, California. It collaborates with MIT. It continues to study Mexico City.

Molina hopes to convince governments to reduce fossil-fuel emissions. This would reduce pollution in the world's cities. He feels this should also reduce global warming. Molina said, "If we take a look at the whole picture, it is clear to me that some strong action needs to be taken on the energy issue."

Mario Molina's work has greatly benefited all of us. He has said, "I am heartened and humbled that I was able to do something that not only contributed to our understanding of atmospheric chemistry, but also had a profound impact on the global environment."

Remembering the Facts

1. How did Mario become interested in science?

2. Why was Mario concerned about his work with chemical lasers?

3. Why were CFCs widely used at one time?

4. What was the subject of Molina's 1974 paper in *Nature*?

5. What did Molina do to get people to pay attention to his findings on CFCs?

6. Why did Mario Molina win the Nobel Prize in 1995?

7. How did he use most of his prize money?

8. What type of center did Molina help set up in 2005?

Understanding the Story

9. Why do you think Mario Molina's work was important enough to win the Nobel Prize?

10. Why do you think air pollution continues to be a world problem today?

Getting the Main Idea

In what ways do you think Mario Molina is a good role model for young Americans?

Applying What You've Learned

Make a list of the causes of air pollution in your city or state.

Bill Richardson
Politician

Bill Richardson has been nominated for the Nobel Peace Prize five times. He has been a member of Congress. He has served as a Cabinet member. He has been ambassador to the United Nations. He has served as governor of New Mexico. He's been a candidate for president of the United States.

Bill's grandfather was from Boston, Massachusetts. He moved to Nicaragua to be a rancher. Bill's father, William B. Richardson, was born in Nicaragua. Bill's father grew up in both Latin America and the United States.

Bill's father became a U.S. citizen. He worked as a banker. He went to Mexico in 1929 to manage a bank. There he met Maria Luisa Lopez-Collada. She was a secretary in the bank. The couple married in 1936. Bill was born on November 15, 1947. He had a younger sister, Vesta.

William wanted his children to be American citizens. Just before each birth, he sent his wife to stay with his sister in Pasadena, California. Thus, both Bill and Vesta became Americans by birth.

The Richardsons were proud to be from Mexico and the United States. They were bilingual. Bill's dad spoke to him in English. His mother talked to him in Spanish. The family celebrated the culture of both countries. They celebrated many different holidays, including Thanksgiving, the Fourth of July, and Mexican Independence Day.

The Richardsons taught their children to be hard workers. Bill's father told him, "If you're going to do something, be the best at it. That usually means you're going to have to work harder than everyone else." The children also learned to give back to their community.

The Richardsons were a wealthy family. Many wealthy families in Mexico City sent their children to private schools. Private schools were filled with kids from diverse backgrounds. Bill went to a public elementary school. He was one of the few, or the only, Mexican Americans in his school. Bill often felt like he didn't fit in. He found it confusing to be "both a Mexican and an American trapped in one body."

Bill was a good student. His real love was baseball. He began playing Little League when he was ten. It soon was clear that he was an excellent player. He was good at pitching and at batting. His father hired Mexican baseball stars to train him. He also began setting up Little League teams all over Mexico.

When Bill was 13, his father sent him to a prep school in the United States. He attended Middlesex School in Concord, Massachusetts. This was near Boston. Bill was the only Hispanic student in the school. Most of the other students were white, upper-class kids. They laughed at Bill's dark skin and poor English. The classes were hard, too. Bill wondered how he was going to make it. He was also homesick. But he couldn't go home to visit. It was just too far.

Things started looking up in the spring. Tryouts were held for the baseball team. Bill Richardson made school history. He was the first 8th grader ever to be a starter on the varsity team. Bill began to win the respect of his classmates.

Scouts from professional baseball teams saw Bill play. They wanted Bill to skip college and play baseball. Bill's father wouldn't let that happen. He told Bill he could play on a college baseball team instead. Bill went to Tufts University in Boston. That was where his father had gone to college. He entered Tufts in 1966.

Bill played baseball on the college team. His plans to play professional baseball after college began to fade. First, Bill began having trouble seeing. He learned that he would have to start wearing glasses. Next, his pitching arm began to go bad. He was no longer able to pitch an entire game.

Bill started to pay more attention to his studies. He majored in political science and French. Bill got his first taste of politics when he was elected president of his fraternity. He found that he liked organizing and planning. He was a good leader. He began to think about a career in public service.

Bill graduated from Tufts in 1970. He decided to go to graduate school. Bill chose the Fletcher School of Law and Diplomacy. Fletcher was on the Tufts campus. Bill earned a master's degree in international affairs.

A group of students from Fletcher went on a trip to Washington, D.C. Senator Hubert Humphrey spoke to them. He told them how he had dedicated his life to fighting poverty and injustice. He said that he felt honored to be part of the U.S. government. He was proud he was in a position to help his fellow citizens.

Bill was inspired by Humphrey's words. He decided that he would devote his life to public service. He said, "I began to realize how a progressive vision could change the world."

Richardson became an unpaid intern for Congressman F. Bradford Morse of Massachusetts. His job was to read committee reports and proposed bills. Then he wrote summaries for Morse to read. The hours were long. The work was often boring. But Richardson learned how to write a clear, accurate summary. He did such a good job that he was offered a full-time job. He was paid $250 a week.

Now that he had a paying job, Richardson asked his girlfriend to marry him. When Bill was 18, he'd met Barbara Flavin. She lived across the street from his high school. They were married in 1972. Sadly, Bill's father died nine days before the wedding.

In 1978, the Richardsons moved to New Mexico. Bill worked as a staff member of the local Democratic Party. He also taught government at Santa Fe Community College.

Richardson decided to run for Congress in 1980. It was his first campaign. He found it was a lot of hard work. He traveled across northern New Mexico. He shook hands with everyone he met. He won the support of local leaders and many voters. But he still lost the election.

Two years later, he tried again. This time he won. Bill Richardson became the youngest freshman member of Congress that year. He was just 35 years old. He represented New Mexico's newly created Third Congressional District. He served in this position for the next 14 years.

Richardson worked hard for the people in his district. He held more than 2,500 town-hall meetings. In a town-hall meeting, citizens gather. They ask their government officials questions. They give their opinions. Officials try to answer their concerns.

Richardson was a member of the Energy and Commerce Committee. He fought for laws to protect the environment. He led the fight to preserve New Mexico's wilderness. Richardson proposed an amendment to the Clean Air Act that would require cleaner gasoline. He encouraged research into ways to prevent oil spills.

Richardson was also on the Interior Committee. This committee focuses on the environment, land use, water use, and Native American affairs. All these are important issues to people in New Mexico. Richardson worked to help Native Americans protect their land. He helped them get better health care and better schools.

Richardson worked hard to set up the world's largest free-trade zone. It included the United States, Canada, and Mexico. It was called the North American Free Trade Agreement (NAFTA). It took effect in 1994. For his work, Richardson was given the Aztec Eagle Award. This is the highest award the Mexican government gives a non-citizen.

Richardson became known as a skilled diplomat. Over the years, he has negotiated for the release of hostages. He secured the release of American servicemen and political prisoners in Cuba, Iraq, and North Korea.

In 1994, North Korea shot down a U.S. Army helicopter. The pilot was captured. Another soldier on board died in the crash. President Clinton asked Richardson to negotiate with the North Koreans to release the pilot. Richardson held days of talks with the North Koreans. Finally, the pilot was released.

In 1995, two American workers were lost in the desert in Iraq. They were arrested as spies. Richardson was sent to Iraq. He met with Iraq's dictator, Saddam Hussein. Hussein did not want to give in. Richardson convinced him to release the men.

In 1997, President Bill Clinton named Bill Richardson to be the U.S. ambassador to the United Nations. In this job, he traveled to Africa on many missions. He went to Zaire to support its efforts to become a democracy. (Zaire is now called the Democratic Republic of the Congo.) He went to Sudan. He worked to release the Red Cross workers held hostage there.

Richardson was greatly affected by his trips to Africa. He saw a great deal of violence, famine, and disease there. He feels that the United States can play an important role in preventing the needless suffering in Africa.

Richardson has worked hard to end suffering around the world. For his efforts, he has been nominated for the Nobel Peace Prize five times.

Richardson has a technique for succeeding in diplomacy. Before each meeting, he sets small goals. He makes sure his objectives are clear. Then he researches the people he will be negotiating with. He tries to be a good listener. He is forceful when presenting what he wants to happen.

In 1998, Richardson became secretary of the U.S. Department of Energy. In this job, he worked for renewable energy. He also worked for tougher energy-efficiency standards. Richardson also worked to secure U.S. nuclear weapons.

In 2002, Richardson ran for governor of New Mexico. He wanted to help his home state solve some of its problems. He was elected in a landslide. He became the only Hispanic-American governor in the 50 states.

Richardson created new jobs. He balanced the state budget. He pushed through a pay raise for teachers. He worked to protect working families of New Mexico. Richardson signed a law saying the state would offer health insurance to every child age five and younger. Minimum wage was increased. Also, New Mexico became the first state to provide $400,000 life-insurance policies to its National Guardsmen on active duty.

Richardson worked to make New Mexico the Clean Energy State. The state became a national leader in the wind, solar, and biofuel industries.

As governor, Richardson continued his diplomatic missions. In 2006, he traveled to Sudan. He negotiated the release of Pulitzer Prize-winning journalist Paul Salopek. Salopek had been working on a story for *National Geographic* magazine. He was falsely arrested as a spy.

In 2006, Bill Richardson was re-elected governor of New Mexico. He won by the largest margin of victory of any governor in New Mexico's history. In 2007, he went back to Sudan. The Save Darfur coalition asked him to meet with President al-Bashir of Sudan and Darfuri rebels. He negotiated a temporary cease-fire between the warring parties.

Richardson was a candidate for president of the United States. He tried to become the 2008 nominee of the Democratic Party. He withdrew from the race after the New Hampshire primary. However, in his campaign, he won the respect of millions of Americans. He was the first Hispanic American to run for America's top job.

Bill Richardson has worked hard all his adult life to make a difference in the United States. In his autobiography, he said, "Long ago, I chose a path. I accepted my duty as an American. I am gratified by the role I have been privileged to play. In small but perhaps significant ways, I have made a difference for my country. Although our challenges as Americans and as citizens of the world are great, we face them together."

Remembering the Facts

1. List two ways Bill recognized the heritage of two cultures as a boy.

2. Why didn't Bill play professional baseball after high school?

3. How did Senator Hubert Humphrey inspire Bill to enter politics?

4. Which congressional district did Richardson represent for 14 years?

5. In what ways did Richardson help Native Americans as part of his work on the Interior Committee?

6. Why was Richardson nominated for the Nobel Peace Prize five times?

7. List three of Richardson's accomplishments as governor of New Mexico.

8. Why is New Mexico known as the Clean Energy State?

Understanding the Story

9. Bill Richardson called his autobiography *Between Worlds.* Why do you think he chose this title?

10. Why do you think Bill Richardson's experiences growing up prepared him for becoming a successful diplomat?

Getting the Main Idea

In what ways do you think Bill Richardson is a good role model for young Americans?

Applying What You've Learned

Make a list of other prominent Hispanic politicians and the states in which they work.

Carlos Santana
Musician

Carlos Santana is a musician. He became popular in the 1960s and 1970s. He is popular with a new generation today. In fact, he won eight Grammy Awards in 2000. He is still making new music. Santana's career has spanned over four decades.

Carlos's band is called Santana. The group is famous for its blend of rock, blues, jazz fusion, and Latin salsa. Carlos himself is known for his beautiful blues-based guitar melodies. He sets these against Latin rhythm instruments such as congas and timbales.

Carlos is more than a great musician. He is a businessman. He is a humanitarian. For many years, he has given his time and money to help others. He also set up the Milagro Foundation. It has given millions of dollars to help needy children.

Carlos Santana was born on July 20, 1947, in Autlán de Navarro, Mexico. His parents were José Santana and Josefina Barragán. Carlos was the fourth of their seven children.

Autlán de Navarro is a tiny, remote village in west central Mexico. The town was very poor. There was no electricity. There was no running water or indoor plumbing. Chickens ran about on the dirt roads.

Most of the men of the village were farmers. José Santana was not. He was a musician. He and his mariachi band played at village events. Mariachi music is a style of Mexican dance music. It is played by small groups using violins and trumpets.

As a boy, Carlos often went with José to his gigs in nearby towns. He saw how José's music brought joy into the hard lives of the villagers. He noticed how José was held in high regard by everyone they met.

When Carlos was five years old, José began teaching him to play the violin. Carlos learned quickly. Soon he played in the church orchestra alongside his father.

The Santanas were strong parents. Carlos said, "From my mother, I learned that everything in life is borrowed from the Lord. From my father, I learned that life is service. From both parents, I learned good manners."

In 1954, José went to Tijuana, Mexico, looking for work. Tijuana is on the border between Mexico and the United States. Many American tourists go to Tijuana. Musicians can find jobs playing in the town's many restaurants and clubs.

A year later, José was still in Tijuana. Josefina hired a cab to take herself and her seven children from Autlán to Tijuana. It was a trip of 1,000 miles! They all settled into a house in downtown Tijuana.

Carlos went to a Catholic elementary school. He went to an after-school program at a local music college. He learned to play classical music such as the works of Mozart and Beethoven. When Carlos got home, his father taught him to play mariachi music.

José decided Carlos was ready to turn professional at age ten. On weekends and after school, Carlos played with his father's mariachi band. José began sending Carlos out on his own to play for tourists.

Carlos was glad he could help his family with his earnings. However, he tired of mariachi music. He had discovered a new kind of music: the blues. His favorite blues artist was B. B. King. At the age of 11, Carlos decided he wanted to play the guitar just like B. B. King.

In 1961, José went to San Francisco looking for work. Not long after José left, Josefina took Carlos to a rock concert. Carlos was thrilled by the electric guitars. He began going to every concert he could. José was glad to hear that Carlos was still interested in music. He mailed Carlos a used electric guitar.

In just a few months, Carlos had learned to play the electric guitar. He joined a band at a club in Tijuana. He played from 4 P.M. to midnight on weekdays. On weekends, he played all night long, until 6 A.M. For this work, Carlos earned $9 a week. After work on Sunday mornings, he went to church to play with the church orchestra. This kept his life in balance.

In 1962, Josefina and the children joined José in San Francisco. They settled in a neighborhood called the Mission District. Many Mexican and Central American immigrants settled there. The area has a history of being ethnically and economically diverse.

When school started in the fall, Carlos was placed in ninth grade. Even though he was 15, his English was too poor for him to go to high school. Two years later, Carlos had improved his English. He enrolled in Mission High School. He soon formed a band with two other students. Soon the group was performing on a regular basis. Carlos graduated in 1965. He became a citizen of the United States that same year.

Many new rock bands were being formed in San Francisco in the mid-1960s. The Fillmore Auditorium was home base for many of them. Some of these rock bands were The Grateful Dead, Jefferson Airplane, Jimi Hendrix, and Janis Joplin's band, Big Brother and the Holding Company.

The Fillmore showcased all kinds of music. Blues singers such as John Lee Hooker were featured. Soul singers such as Aretha Franklin appeared. Carlos tried to go to every show the Fillmore offered. He worked as a dishwasher at a drive-in so he could buy tickets.

In 1966, Carlos and five other young men formed the Santana Blues Band. The group had a new sound. They blended rock, blues, and jazz.

They added a Latin conga rhythm that made them unique. Soon the band became known simply as Santana. By 1968, the group was a San Francisco favorite.

In 1969, Santana signed a recording contract with Columbia Records. Their first album was named *Santana*. Before the album was released, Santana played at the Woodstock music festival, in August 1969. It was an outdoor concert near the town of Woodstock, New York. All the top bands in the country played in the three-day concert. Nearly 500,000 people were there.

Santana took the stage on Saturday afternoon. They played several numbers in front of the lively crowd. Their last song was "Soul Sacrifice." The song continued for a full ten minutes. The crowd had never heard anything like it. They jumped to their feet and gave Santana a standing ovation!

When the album *Santana* was released two months later, it was a huge hit. After just a few months on the market, it was close to double platinum. (That means nearly two million records sold.) The single "Evil Ways" was a Top-10 single.

Santana released its second album, *Abraxas*, in 1970. It was the top-selling album in the country for six weeks. Two songs on the album were Top-10 hits. They were "Black Magic Woman" and "Oye Como Va." Many music critics consider *Abraxas* to be the best album Carlos Santana ever made. Some think it is one of the best rock albums ever recorded.

In 1971, the band recorded their third album. *Santana III* was also well received by music critics. The album had a strong Latin tone.

The original Santana band broke up in 1972. There had been many problems leading to the break-up. Many of the band members were taking illegal drugs. Carlos himself had used marijuana and LSD.

At this point, Carlos had become discouraged with the rock-and-roll lifestyle. The drugs were damaging his life. He felt that he had reached a dead end. He decided he needed to go in other directions with his music and with his life.

He became interested in jazz. He especially liked a new kind of jazz called fusion. Fusion was a mix of rock and jazz. Carlos formed a new group of musicians. The group kept the name Santana. They created an album called *Caravanserai* in the fusion style.

In the summer of 1972, Carlos met Deborah King. The couple married in 1973. They had three children, Salvador, Stella, and Angelica.

The couple became followers of an Indian poet and guru named Sri Chinmoy. He taught his followers to stay away from drugs, alcohol, and tobacco. He taught them about exercise and meditation. Carlos and Deborah became vegetarians. They gave up drugs and alcohol. They began running marathons.

Carlos made several albums that were inspired by the guru's teachings. None of these was very popular with his fans. His major success of the mid-1970s was the album *Santana's Greatest Hits*. This was a collection of the old band's songs.

By 1981, Carlos and Deborah had grown tired of the guru. They looked for inspiration elsewhere. They eventually explored Christianity.

In 1997, Carlos and his band signed a contract with Arista Records. It seemed that the time was right for him to make a comeback. Other singers such as Gloria Estefan, Jennifer Lopez, Ricky Martin, and Marc Anthony had brought Latin music back to the country's attention.

Carlos was inducted into the Rock and Roll Hall of Fame in 1998. Soon afterward, he began recording the album *Supernatural*. Half of the album was done in the classic Santana Latin rock style. The other half paired Carlos with younger, popular musicians. It took almost a year to complete the album.

It was worth it. The album quickly sold 15 million copies in the United States. It sold 25 million more copies worldwide. It was the best-selling album ever made by a Hispanic-American musician. The album swept the 2000 Grammy Awards. It won eight Grammys in all, including Album of the Year.

In 2002, Carlos made the album *Shaman* in the same style. Just a month later, the album had gone double platinum. Carlos now had fans of all ages, including many teenagers and their parents.

In 2004, Carlos was honored as the Latin Academy of Recording Arts and Sciences Person of the Year. In 2005, he was honored as a BMI Icon at the BMI Latin Awards. (BMI stands for Broadcast Music, Inc. It is a group of 300,000 American composers, songwriters, and music publishers.)

In 2005, Carlos released two more albums. These were *Possibilities* and *All That I Am*. In 2006, he toured Europe. He was the opening act for his son Salvador Santana's band. In 2007, he appeared on Gloria Estefan's album *90 Millas*.

Carlos is more than a great musician. From the very beginning of his music career, he supported charities. He is generous with his money and his time. In 1985, he performed in the benefit concert Live Aid. This concert raised millions of dollars for victims of famine in Africa. He supported countless other charities in the 1970s and 1980s.

In 1998, Carlos and Deborah started their own nonprofit group. It is called the Milagro Foundation. (Milagro is Spanish for "miracle.") The purpose of Milagro is to help children around the world. Milagro supports groups that work for children's health, education, and the arts.

Carlos Santana funds Milagro almost entirely by himself. He gives part of the profits from each album and concert ticket he sells to the group. He and Deborah have also designed lines of women's shoes and fragrances. All the profits from these go into the foundation. Carlos has given more than $2 million in grants to various humanitarian agencies.

Carlos's adult life has not been free of sadness. In November 2007, Deborah filed for divorce from Carlos. In an October 2008 interview with *Rolling Stone* magazine, Carlos spoke about the painful separation. "The thing I learned is, you have to go through the darkest night of the soul to get to the brightest light of the day, and that's what I did last year."

Even so, Carlos still helps others. Carlos says, "We all have a part to play in making this a better world.... We need to give back from whatever success we've been blessed to have. Success isn't about being top on the charts or having a lot of money. It's about being good at whatever you do and finding a way to help other people along the way."

Remembering the Facts

1. How did Carlos learn to play the violin?

2. What is mariachi music?

3. Why did Carlos decide he wanted to play the guitar?

4. Why was San Francisco a good place for a young musician in the 1960s?

5. Why was the Woodstock festival so important in Carlos's career?

6. Why did Carlos decide to change his lifestyle in 1972?

7. What kind of music did the *Supernatural* album feature?

8. What is the purpose of the Milagro Foundation?

Understanding the Story

9. Explain how the teachings of his parents inspired Carlos to lead a balanced life in the world of a rock musician.

10. Explain how Carlos Santana's style of music differs from that of other rock musicians.

Getting the Main Idea

In what ways do you think Carlos Santana is a good role model for young Americans?

Applying What You've Learned

Think about the kinds of music you enjoy. Put two or more of them together to "create" a new kind of music. Give your music a name. Explain how it would sound.

Antonia Hernandez
Civil-Rights Lawyer

The Mexican American Legal Defense and Educational Fund is known as MALDEF. It is the leading Hispanic civil-rights group in the United States. Its mission is to protect the rights of 45 million Hispanic Americans.

MALDEF was founded in 1968 in San Antonio, Texas. It works on a variety of issues that affect Hispanic Americans. It works for better education for Hispanic Americans. It works to provide job training. It fights to make sure that voting districts are fairly drawn.

Antonia Hernandez was president and general counsel (lawyer) for MALDEF from 1985 to 2003. She has worked hard for the rights of Hispanics. "We are the Hispanic community's law firm," she says.

Antonia Hernandez was born on May 30, 1948, in Torreón, Mexico. She was the oldest of seven children.

Antonia's mother, Nicolasa, grew up on a ranch in Mexico. Her father, Manuel, was an American citizen. He was born in Texas during the Great Depression. There was very little work available at that time in Texas. So the U.S. government sent Manuel's family and many other Mexican Americans to Mexico. In Mexico, Manuel met Nicolasa. They were later married.

In 1956, when Antonia was eight, her parents moved their family to the United States. They wanted their children to get a good education.

They settled in East Los Angeles. Manuel was a gardener and laborer. Nicolasa stayed home to raise the children. She took part-time jobs when she could.

Antonia's parents encouraged all their children to do well in school. They also showed the children the importance of being kind and helping others.

Antonia worked hard to help her family. She took care of her siblings when her parents were at work. She sold her mother's homemade tamales to earn money. When she grew older, she worked at produce stands. In the summers, the entire family worked picking crops.

The Hernandez family taught their children to be proud of their Mexican roots. Antonia has said, "When I came to the United States, I was very proud of who I was. I was a Mexican. I had an identity. I had been taught a history, a culture of centuries of rich civilization." Antonia was proud to be a Hispanic American.

When Antonia started school, she spoke only Spanish. She was placed in a class with a teacher who spoke only English. She endured a lot of teasing from the other students. They laughed at her clothing and her hairstyle. School was hard until Antonia finally learned enough English to get by. She became an excellent student.

From a young age, Antonia knew she wanted to dedicate her life to helping others. While still in her early teens, she marched in picket lines to support California's farm workers.

Antonia knew she wanted to go to college. She began at a local community college. Then she went on to the University of California, Los Angeles (UCLA). She earned her degree in history in 1970. Then she got her teaching certificate in 1971.

Antonia Hernandez began working in a teen counseling program in the ghetto. Soon she decided she knew a better way to help kids and teachers. She wanted to do something about the unfair laws that discriminated against minorities.

Hernandez decided to become a lawyer. She went to law school at UCLA. In law school, she joined some Hispanic student groups. She worked on issues that affected minority students.

She graduated from law school in 1974. She went to work as a lawyer for the Los Angeles Center for Law and Justice. Then she became directing attorney for the Legal Aid Foundation's office in Lincoln Heights. Legal-aid lawyers provide free legal help for poor people. She also fought for pro-minority bills in the state legislature.

In 1977, she married Michael Stern, who was also a lawyer. The couple later had three children.

In 1978, Hernandez was offered a new job. She would be staff counsel (lawyer) for the U.S. Senate Judiciary Committee under Senator Ted Kennedy. She turned down the job. She was happy doing legal-aid work to help the poor people of Los Angeles. She really didn't want to leave her hometown.

The committee couldn't believe that she had turned down the job because she loved her legal-aid work. They thought the real reason must be the salary. So they offered her more money.

Hernandez turned down the job again. But her husband finally talked her into it. He told her it was a career move that was too good to pass up.

Hernandez and her husband moved to Washington, D.C. She became the first Hispanic American to serve as staff counsel to the U.S. Senate Committee on the Judiciary. She advised the committee on immigration and human-rights issues.

Hernandez worked to extend the Voting Rights Act. She fought for bilingual voting assistance. ("Bilingual" means that a person can speak two languages equally well.) This assistance helps those who don't yet know English well to understand the voting process.

Hernandez worked for the committee for two years. But then in 1980, the Democrats lost control of the Senate. That meant that the Republicans would take over the Judiciary Committee. Antonia Hernandez was out of a job.

A few days later, she had a job offer from the Mexican American Legal Defense and Educational Fund. She joined its Washington, D.C., office. She quickly worked her way up through the ranks. In 1985, she was elected president and general counsel. She directed the nine MALDEF offices across the country.

While working with MALDEF, Hernandez was able to get many laws passed to help Hispanic Americans. She fought for fair funding for public schools. She went to court to make sure school-district lines were drawn fairly. She worked to get more jobs for Hispanic Americans.

She worked to make sure voting districts were formed fairly. That way, Hispanic Americans would have a better chance of getting elected to political office. She fought against a bill that would have required Hispanics to carry I.D. cards. She said this would lead to discrimination.

MALDEF worked to prevent the nominations of federal judges who had poor records on civil-rights issues. The group also fought against Proposition 187. This bill would have denied free public education and health benefits to illegal immigrants and their children. The bill was struck down by a federal court.

MALDEF also taught Hispanic Americans to serve on boards that make policy. It provided education to parents. It helped them become leaders in their local schools. Parents were also taught how to advocate for what their children needed to succeed in school.

Hernandez has worked hard for bilingual education. Many Hispanics speak Spanish as their first language. Later they learn English.

Hernandez believes strongly in bilingual education. There are different models for bilingual education. Most programs teach children in their native language for up to three years. That way they do not fall behind in their math, science, and social studies classes. They also learn English. Later they go on to regular classes taught only in English.

Bilingual education is controversial. It can be costly. Some say it doesn't work any better than just putting children into regular classrooms. Hernandez admits that she was able to learn English with no extra help. But some children don't make it this way. They become frustrated and drop out of school. Hernandez wants to make sure that all children have a good chance to get an education.

Living in Washington, D.C., made Hernandez more aware of the different groups of Hispanic Americans. In Los Angeles, where she grew up, most Hispanic Americans are Mexican. On the East Coast, she met Puerto Ricans, Cubans, and South and Central Americans. This gave her a broader view of Hispanic Americans and their needs.

Hernandez has worked for unity among civil-rights groups. She worked with the NAACP, the largest African-American civil-rights group. They worked together on the 1991 Civil Rights Act. She believes that all minority groups should work together for a stronger America.

In *Time* magazine, Hernandez said, "By acknowledging the contributions made to our country by Native Americans and by Hispanics and blacks and Asians, we're really strengthening our unity." Hernandez feels that all these groups have made vital contributions to what our country is today.

In 2004, Hernandez became president and CEO of the California Community Foundation (CCF). The purpose of the CCF is to improve life for the poor people of Los Angeles. The group works for safe, decent housing. It seeks to make health care available. It works for better education. It also supports the arts and cultural activities.

The CCF achieves its goals by connecting a variety of worthy programs with people who wish to donate money. It helps donors give money to non-profit groups that work to improve the lives of poor people. The foundation is the ninth largest community foundation in the United States.

Hernandez has said, "What I truly want is for every person to have the opportunity to fulfill his or her potential. Being able to create an opportunity for people of wealth to share their resources with those in need is wonderful. We're creating a community in which we're all interdependent. It's what makes this country so great."

A 2008 study funded by the CCF showed that nearly half the workers in Los Angeles are foreign-born. Nearly one-third of adults in L.A. are in the process of learning to speak English. And 40 percent of the children in L.A. schools are English Language Learners.

This means that there is much work left to be done. Many of these millions of immigrants will need help to become part of American society. Hernandez said, "The only way we can tap immigrants' full potential … is through social integration, economic mobility, educational opportunity, and civic engagement."

Hernandez has won many awards for her work. In 1996, she was one in the first group of lawyers to win the Spirit of Excellence Award from the American Bar Association. The motto of the award is "To the Stars Through Difficulty." Antonia Hernandez has overcome many difficulties in her life. But through hard work and dedication to her values, she has made a difference in the lives of many Americans.

Remembering the Facts

1. What civil rights group did Hernandez lead from 1985 to 2003?

2. Name two reasons school was difficult for Antonia at first.

3. How did Antonia help her family as a teen?

4. Why did Antonia Hernandez decide to become a lawyer?

5. What type of work did Hernandez do for the Senate Judiciary Committee?

6. List three areas MALDEF has worked on.

7. What job did Hernandez take in 2004?

8. What is the purpose of the CCF?

Understanding the Story

9. Why do you think bilingual education is a controversial topic?

10. Why do you think Hernandez feels that all minority groups should work together?

Getting the Main Idea

In what ways do you think Antonia Hernandez is a good role model for young Americans?

Applying What You've Learned

Imagine that you have enrolled in a school in another country. You do not speak that language, and your teacher and classmates do not speak English. Write a paragraph explaining the difficulties you would face.

Gloria Estefan
Singer

Gloria Estefan is a famous singer. She is known as the Queen of Latin Pop. She has won five Grammy Awards. She has sold over 70 million albums and CDs. Estefan is also known for her many works of charity. She has used her fame and wealth to make the world a better place.

Estefan's story is also one of struggle and tragedy. With hard work, she has overcome her troubles. She has used these troubles to inspire her music. Through it all, she has stayed true to her roots and values.

Gloria Estefan was born Gloria Marie Fajardo on September 1, 1957, in Havana, Cuba. Her father, José, was a security guard. His job was to protect the president of Cuba, General Fulgencio Batista. Gloria's mother was a teacher. Gloria also had a younger sister, Becky.

When Gloria was a year old, Fidel Castro overthrew Batista's government. Castro set up a communist government. He got rid of Batista's supporters. Some were thrown in prison. Others were killed. Gloria's father was in prison for five months. When he got out, people were afraid to hire him.

Gloria's parents knew they had to leave Cuba. But they didn't want the government to find out. Cuba is only 90 miles away from Florida. Florida had always been a popular destination for Cubans. The family bought round-trip tickets to Miami, Florida. They pretended that they were just going to visit friends.

The family thought they might be able to return to Cuba in a few months. They never could. Gloria still has her unused return ticket.

Many other Cubans had fled Cuba. A lot of them settled in Miami. The part of town where they lived became known as Little Havana. The Fajardos found a small apartment. It was a big change from their large home in Cuba.

The Cuban refugees wanted Castro out of power. The U.S. government did, too. It was threatened by having a communist government so close to the U.S. mainland.

The U.S. CIA (Central Intelligence Agency) made plans to invade Cuba. About 1,300 Cuban refugees volunteered to fight with U.S. support. Gloria's father was among them. They traveled by boat and landed at the Bay of Pigs in Cuba. The plan failed. Many men were killed. Gloria's father was taken prisoner. He was freed 18 months later.

José Fajardo joined the U.S. Army. He could do so because of his service in Cuba. The family moved to San Antonio, Texas. Gloria was the only child in the first grade who spoke Spanish. She quickly learned to speak English.

On Gloria's ninth birthday, her mother gave her a guitar. She also signed Gloria up for classical guitar lessons. Gloria hated the lessons. She wanted to play music like the music she heard on the radio. Gloria taught herself to play the popular tunes of the day.

Gloria's father went to fight in the Vietnam War in 1966. When he returned in 1968, he began having health problems. His illness affected his nervous system. Soon José couldn't walk or take care of himself. Eleven-year-old Gloria had to take care of him. She did so for the next five years.

Gloria's mother worked to support the family. She also went to night school to get a teaching degree. When Gloria was 16, José was placed in a veterans' hospital.

Music was the one thing that got Gloria through those difficult years. She later said, "Music was my escape. It was my release from everything. I'd lock myself up in my room with my guitar. I would sing for hours by myself." Gloria wrote songs about her family and about being a teenager. She sang them to herself over and over.

In 1975, Gloria attended a wedding. She was 17 years old. The band at the wedding was the Miami Latin Boys. Emilio Estefan led the band. He and his family were also Cuban refugees.

Emilio had heard that Gloria could sing. He asked her to perform with the band. They sounded good together. Emilio asked Gloria to join the group. She began singing with the band on weekends. During the week, she attended the University of Miami. She majored in communications and psychology.

When Gloria joined the band, she felt awkward. She describes herself then as "a lumpy, fat teenager with one big eyebrow and huge cheeks." She was very shy. When she sang, she stared at the floor. Emilio helped Gloria overcome her stage fright. He encouraged her to work out and to dress better. Gloria watched tapes of herself performing. She worked hard to gain confidence.

The band changed its name to the Miami Sound Machine. They played at parties nearly every weekend. Gloria learned to sing different kinds of music. She sang pop, rock, rhythm and blues, and soul. She sang Cuban and South American songs. All this stretched her range as a performer.

The group produced its first album, *Renacer (Live Again),* in 1977. On one side of the record, the songs were sung in English. On the other side, they were sung in Spanish.

The year 1978 was a good one for Gloria. She graduated with honors from the University of Miami. She also married Emilio Estefan.

In 1980, the couple had a son. They named him Nayib ("good person"). Gloria brought Nayib to rehearsals and on tour.

That same year, the Miami Sound Machine signed with CBS Records. Between 1980 and 1984, they made four albums in Spanish. Few of the albums were sold in the United States. But they were huge hits in Latin American countries.

In 1984, the group signed a contract with Epic Records. Emilio wanted to record songs for the English-language market. The group's first song in English was "Dr. Beat." The song sold well. So next the group released an entire album in English, *Eyes of Innocence.*

Their next album, *Primitive Love,* was their first gold record. It had three Top-10 hits. Estefan had written two of them. One of the songs was "Conga." This song was the first song in music history to appear on Billboard magazine's dance, R&B, and Latin charts at the same time. Gloria Estefan and the Miami Sound Machine were now known around the world!

In 1987, Emilio stopped performing with the band. He became the band's manager full time. He wrote songs for the group. He worked on producing the albums. He organized the group's touring schedule.

The band's name was changed to Gloria Estefan and the Miami Sound Machine. They toured seven countries. Everywhere they went the concerts were sold out.

In Cuba, however, the group was banned. Castro's government ordered that their albums could not be sold. Their songs could not be played on the radio. Still, some people managed to get the albums into the country. Estefan dreams that someday she will be able to perform in her homeland.

In 1989, the album *Cuts Both Ways* featured Gloria Estefan's name as soloist on the cover. That year, she won the American Billboard Award for Songwriter of the Year. The Miami Sound Machine won the American Music Award as the favorite pop/rock band of the year.

Estefan began to use her fame to help others. She worked hard on a campaign to keep young people off drugs. Her picture was seen on billboards all over the country. The billboards read, "If you need someone, call a friend. Don't do drugs."

The city of Miami was proud of Gloria and Emilio Estefan. The mayor gave the couple the key to the city. The street on which they lived was renamed. The new name was Miami Sound Machine Boulevard.

In March 1990, Estefan and her family were riding in a tour bus. They were traveling to Syracuse, New York. Estefan planned to do a concert there.

The weather was bad. The road was icy. A truck crashed into the tour bus. Estefan broke a vertebra (bone) in her back. Surgeons put eight-inch rods on both sides of her broken vertebra. Then they fused her spine together. She had 400 stitches.

Estefan was unable to walk. She had difficulty with even simple tasks, such as brushing her teeth. It took a long time and a lot of hard work for Estefan to recover. She had six hours of physical therapy three days a week for an entire year.

All her work paid off. Just a year later, she opened her Into the Light tour. The first number she performed was "Get on Your Feet!" The tour continued to nine countries. More than five million people heard Estefan perform.

In August 1992, Hurricane Andrew hit the coast of Florida. The Estefans' home was spared. But more than 300,000 people were left homeless.

Estefan jumped in to help. She sent a $100,000 check to United Way's hurricane relief fund. She and Emilio collected clothing for hurricane victims. They organized a benefit concert. They raised $4 million for the hurricane relief fund. Estefan made a music video called "Always Tomorrow." All the proceeds from the sales of the video went to hurricane relief.

In 1992, Estefan released her *Greatest Hits.* The album went platinum. That meant it sold more than 1 million copies.

Estefan has won many awards. In 1993, she was awarded a star on the Hollywood Walk of Fame. (Emilio got his star in 2005.) Also in 1993, she was given the Ellis Island Congressional Medal of Honor. That is a high honor given to a citizen who was not born in the United States.

Estefan's 1993 album *Mi Tierra* was in Spanish. Some people worried that the album would not sell well. They told her, "You're too Latin for the Americans and too American for the Latins." Estefan replied, "But that's who I am. I'm Cuban American. I'm not one thing or the other." *Mi Tierra* earned Estefan her first Grammy Award. She was named artist of the year at the Latin Music Awards.

In 1994, Gloria and Emilio had their second child. They named their daughter Emily Marie Estefan.

In 1995, the Estefans were boating on Biscayne Bay in Florida. A jet ski cut in front of them. Then it turned and crashed into their boat. Sadly, the young driver was thrown from his jet ski. He died.

Gloria Estefan wanted to make some good come out of the tragedy. She worked to make Florida's boating safety laws stronger. Training was put in place for the users of jet skis. All boaters under 16 must now take a safety course before they can drive a boat.

In 1996, Estefan recorded the album *Destiny.* She wrote most of the songs for the album. One of the songs, "Reach," was the official song of the 1996 Summer Olympic Games in Atlanta, Georgia. Estefan performed the song at the closing ceremony of those Olympics.

In 1996, Estefan was inducted into the National Academy of Popular Music's Songwriters Hall of Fame. She was given the Hitmaker Award. That same year she received *Billboard* magazine's first Spirit of Hope award. Estefan won the award for her charity work.

Estefan played a part in the movie *Music of the Heart.* The movie was about a teacher trying to bring music education to the schools of New York. Estefan believes that music is important for every child's development.

Gloria and Emilio Estefan were honored with the Sammy Cahn Lifetime Achievement Award in 2001. The award was from the National Academy of Popular Music. They were the first Hispanics to receive this award.

Estefan released the album *Unwrapped* in 2003. After that, she took time off from music to do other things. In 2005, she published her first children's book. She and her husband opened several restaurants.

In 2006, Estefan released *The Essential Gloria Estefan.* This two-disc set contained most of her biggest hits from 1984 to 2003. All her Spanish greatest hits were released on the album *Oye Mi Canto! Los Exitos.* In 2007, she recorded another Spanish album, *90 Millas.*

This new album did very well at the 2008 Latin Grammy Awards. *90 Millas* won for Best Traditional Tropical Album. "Pintame de Colores," a song from the album, won for Best Tropical Song. Gloria Estefan was named the 2008 Latin Grammy Person of the Year.

Gloria and Emilio Estefan have continued to work to help other people. They set up the Gloria Estefan Foundation. All the royalties from three of Estefan's songs go into the foundation. Estefan's fans give money to the foundation on her birthday each year. The foundation gives about $500,000 a year to various charities.

Gloria Estefan has been an entertainer since the 1970s. She still performs. She had a successful world tour in 2008. She continues to play an important role in bringing the Latin sound to popular music. She paved the way for other Hispanic-American stars.

Estefan says that she has the best of both worlds. She said in an interview with *Time,* "I have a Cuban heart and an American head. It's a good balance."

Remembering the Facts

1. Why did the Fajardo family decide to leave Cuba?

2. What was the purpose of the Bay of Pigs invasion?

3. Why did Gloria have to take care of her father for five years?

4. How did the song "Conga" make music history?

5. How was Estefan injured in 1990?

6. List two ways Gloria and Emilio helped the victims of Hurricane Andrew.

7. What is the importance of the Ellis Island Congressional Medal of Honor?

8. What is the purpose of the Gloria Estefan Foundation?

Understanding the Story

9. How do you think Estefan used her music as a way to work through her various troubles during her life?

10. Why do you think the government of Cuba does not allow Estefan's CDs to be sold or played in the country?

Getting the Main Idea

In what ways do you think Gloria Estefan is a good role model for young Americans?

Applying What You've Learned

Think of a problem you have in your life right now. Write some words for a short song expressing your feelings about this problem. Put your words to music if you like.

Edgar Prado
Jockey

Edgar Prado is one of America's most successful horse-racing jockeys. In 2008, he became the 16th jockey in U.S. history to win 6,000 races. He is a member of the National Museum of Racing Hall of Fame.

Prado has all the characteristics needed to be a great jockey. He is fearless. He is intelligent and can make quick decisions. He loves horses. A horse that senses it is loved will be willing to do what it is told. That is how races are won. Prado won national fame as jockey for the beloved racehorse Barbaro.

Edgar was born on June 12, 1967, in Lima, Peru. He was the tenth of eleven children (and the youngest of eight boys). His father, Jose, had wanted to be a jockey. But he couldn't keep his weight low enough. So Jose became a racehorse trainer instead. Edgar's mother, Zenaida, cared for the large family. She took in odd jobs when she could.

Jose was not well paid for his work. So the family was extremely poor. They all lived in a one-bedroom house with no electricity. The single bedroom was lined with bunk beds. Everyone shared one bathroom.

Jose loved his work with horses. He never even thought of taking a higher-paying job. Every morning he would get up at 4 A.M. and go to work at the racetrack. If anything was wrong with one of the horses under his care, he would sleep all night in its stall. He had to be sure the horse would be OK. Sometimes young Edgar would stay with him.

Edgar's mother worked hard taking care of her large family. Edgar later said that he got his work ethic from her. "She was an inspiration in my life. She gave me a lot of support. She really made me the person that I am."

Edgar also became a hard worker. When he was five, he cleaned out horse stables. At seven, he sold fruit on the streets.

Edgar loved horses and racing from an early age. Two of his older brothers were jockeys. Edgar longed to ride fast horses, too. It didn't even scare him when his brothers fell off the horses.

Edgar took a job exercising horses when he was 14. At 15, he began to race them. By the time he was 17, he was the top jockey in Peru.

In high school, Edgar had planned to become a lawyer. Now he decided to give a career as a jockey a shot. To do this, he would need to move to the United States. So in 1986, 18-year-old Edgar moved to Miami, Florida.

Life in the United States was not easy for Edgar Prado. He didn't know anyone. He couldn't drive a car, so it wasn't easy getting around. He didn't speak any English.

Prado stood 5 feet 4 inches tall and weighed 113 pounds. His small size was just right for being a jockey. But since he spoke only Spanish, many trainers would not hire him to ride. The only jobs he got were riding horses that were old or slow. He told his mother about his lack of progress. She kept telling him, "Keep fighting, son."

Prado had his first win on American soil on June 1, 1986. He rode the horse Single Love at Miami's Calder Race Course. After that he had more successes. He made enough money to move three of his siblings to the United States.

In 1988, Prado hired Steve Rushing as his agent. Rushing recognized Prado's special ability to work with horses. He said, "You can't teach (a jockey) to communicate with a horse. Some people have it; some people don't. Edgar definitely, definitely has it."

Prado said, "I can spend five minutes with a horse in the warm-up before a race and tell you its strengths, weaknesses, likes, and dislikes. A good jockey listens to a horse breathe, feels him as he moves."

Horse racing is more popular in Maryland than Florida. So in 1989, Prado moved to Maryland. Three years later, he had become the top jockey in Maryland. He led the United States in victories for three straight years.

In 1989, Edgar married his childhood sweetheart, Lilliana. The two had been neighbors back in Peru. They had three children named Edgar Jr., Patricia, and Luis. Edgar and Lilliana both became U.S. citizens in 1993.

One of the largest horse-racing centers in the United States is in New York. Edgar Prado decided to move his family to New York in 1999.

Prado began to win major races. In 2002, he won the Belmont Stakes. He rode a horse named Sarava. The odds against Sarava winning were higher than 70 to 1. Yet Prado rode him to victory.

In 2004, Prado won the Belmont Stakes again. This time he rode a horse named Birdstone. Again, they were the underdogs. They beat a horse named Smarty Jones who was heavily favored to win. That same year, Prado rode Birdstone to victory at the Travers Stakes at the Saratoga Race Track in Saratoga Springs, New York.

In 2005, Prado won two Breeders' Cup races. He rode Folklore in the Breeders' Cup Juvenile Fillies. Then he won again on Silver Train in the Breeders' Cup Sprint.

There was one special horse Prado had longed to ride: Barbaro. Barbaro was a powerful two-year-old thoroughbred. He was more than 5 ½ feet tall and solid muscle.

Prado liked Barbaro right away. He felt that Barbaro could sense his affection. The two hit it off. On New Year's Day 2006, Prado rode Barbaro in the Tropical Park Derby in Miami. They won by four lengths.

Prado said, "His running style was so smooth that I felt like I was flying." The two raced again in February and April. By this time, Barbaro had won five races in a row. The next stop was the Kentucky Derby.

Prado had ridden on other horses in the Derby six times without a win. He knew that Barbaro had a great shot at winning. The horse was a born champion. He was big and tough. He had great speed and endurance. Prado hoped for a victory!

The race was held on May 6, 2006. It took place at Churchill Downs in Louisville, Kentucky. The crowd waited in anticipation for what was sure to be an exciting race. When it was time for the race to begin, Prado got on the horse. He walked Barbaro out to the track. As they went, Prado patted the horse. He told him, "You're a good boy. Are you ready to run? I know you are."

Twenty horses were loaded into the starting gate. When the gate opened, Barbaro stumbled. But he didn't fall. He got his balance back and was off!

Barbaro was three or four lengths behind the leaders. Prado guided him to a spot where he could run smoothly and relax.

When they rounded the far turn, Prado gave Barbaro the signal to speed up. Barbaro passed the other horses effortlessly. They appeared to be slowing to a walk as Barbaro whizzed by. Barbaro took the lead.

At first, Barbaro seemed not to understand why no other horses were in front of him. He slowed down. Prado gave him the signal to run. Then Barbaro knew that he should run as fast as he could. Prado later said it felt like "being in a car going from zero to 60 mph in a matter of seconds."

The crowd went wild. The announcer yelled, "It's all Barbaro! It's all Barbaro!" And indeed it was. The other horses were racing for second place.

Barbaro was excited to be going at top speed. His lead grew and grew. Barbaro and Prado flew across the finish line in first place. They had won the Kentucky Derby by 6 ½ lengths! It was the largest margin of victory at the Derby since 1946. Barbaro became a national hero.

An NBC reporter, Donna Brothers, asked Prado how he felt about the victory. He said, "I was very, very confident today. In America, dreams come true."

Two weeks later, another big race was held. It was the Preakness Stakes at Pimlico Race Course in Baltimore, Maryland. Everyone was talking about Barbaro. They thought he had a good chance of winning the race. If he did, he might go on to become the first Triple Crown winner in 28 years.

The Triple Crown is a series of thoroughbred horse races. It includes the Kentucky Derby, the Preakness Stakes, and the Belmont Stakes. In 132 years, only 11 horses have won the Triple Crown. Barbaro was highly favored to be the 12th.

It's very difficult to become a Triple Crown winner. That's because the three races are so close together. The 1¼-mile-long Kentucky Derby is held the first Saturday in May. The Preakness Stakes is just two weeks later. It's 1 ³⁄₁₆ mile long. Then the 1½-mile-long Belmont Stakes is three weeks after that. Running these three races so close together is a big strain on a horse.

The day of the Preakness Stakes was beautiful. Barbaro looked ready to run. As the horses approached the loading gate, some people in the crowd saw Prado look down at Barbaro's right rear leg. They wondered if Barbaro was OK. But it seemed that he was. Prado loaded Barbaro into the starting gate.

Then the trouble began. Barbaro heard a click and thought it was time to start running. He kicked open his gate and began to run down the track. It was a false start. Barbaro had to be stopped and then reloaded in the starting gate.

Prado and the track vet looked Barbaro over carefully. He seemed fine, so the race went on. Barbaro took right off with the other horses.

About 100 yards down the track, Prado felt Barbaro weaken. He feared that the horse had pulled a muscle. He jumped down and led the horse off the track right away. Barbaro stood with his right hind foot raised off the dirt. Prado knew instantly it was a serious injury. He leaned his shoulder into the horse's shoulder to support Barbaro.

The vet X-rayed Barbaro's leg. It was broken in at least two dozen places. Barbaro's racing career was over. Prado's quick action on the track had saved his life.

Often when a horse's leg is broken, he will be put down (killed in a humane way). Barbaro's owners did not want to end Barbaro's life. Barbaro went to an animal hospital in Pennsylvania. He went into surgery to put his leg back together. It took more than 20 screws and a plate. Then the leg was put into a cast.

After that, things seemed to be going well. Barbaro ate well and seemed to be content. But the vet continued to watch him closely. He knew that at any time, complications could develop.

Prado drove down from New York to see Barbaro many times. Barbaro would put his head on Prado's shoulder. Prado could tell how the horse was feeling.

For months, Barbaro fought his injuries. Then he developed a serious hoof disease called laminitis. It could not be cured. On January 29, 2007, Barbaro had to be put to sleep. Prado was devastated.

Racing was Prado's life and career. So he kept on riding other horses in other races. But he felt that he and Barbaro would always have a very special bond. Prado had loved and admired the horse more than any other he had ridden.

Barbaro had won the hearts of millions of Americans. He also made Prado famous. Prado became known as a man of great compassion and love for his animals. His quick thinking on the track that day was widely thought to have saved Barbaro's life at the time.

Edgar Prado has received many special awards for his racing. Prado won the All-Star Jockey Championship in both 2000 and 2003. He received the Fourstardave Award in both 2002 and 2005. This award honors special achievement at Saratoga Race Course in New York. He won the George Woolf Memorial Jockey Award in 2003. He earned the Eclipse Award for Outstanding Jockey in 2006.

On September 24, 2006, Prado was awarded the New York Racing Association's 2006 Mike Venezia Memorial Award. Jockeys, writers, and fans vote to decide the winner of this award. It is given to a person who exemplifies "extraordinary sportsmanship and citizenship."

On April 21, 2008, Edgar Prado was chosen to be inducted into the National Museum of Racing Hall of Fame.

Edgar Prado is a longtime supporter of Belmont Park's Anna House. This is a day-care center for children of families who work in the racing industry. Anna House provides a scholarship fund for children who qualify.

Edgar Prado gives most of the credit for his success as a jockey to the horses he rides. He said, "It took a lot of hard work and a lot of good horses to take me there. You cannot go to the Indy 500 riding a Honda. In order to show you can ride, you have to have the ammunition to do it." In an interview with NPR, Prado said, "Barbaro was the teammate of a lifetime." Prado wrote about his life and his special bond with Barbaro in his 2008 book, *My Guy Barbaro.*

Remembering the Facts

1. Why did Edgar love horses from a young age?

2. How did Edgar's mother inspire him?

3. What special ability does Edgar Prado have that makes him a great jockey?

4. Why did Prado decide to move from Maryland to New York?

5. What race did Barbaro win on May 6, 2006?

6. What is the Triple Crown?

7. What happened at the Preakness Stakes to end Barbaro's career?

8. What does Prado say is the key to his success as a jockey?

Understanding the Story

9. Why do you think Barbaro won the hearts of millions of Americans?

10. Why do you think being a jockey is a dangerous occupation?

Getting the Main Idea

In what ways do you think Edgar Prado is a good role model for young Americans?

Applying What You've Learned

Write a paragraph, write a poem, or draw a picture to show how you think it would feel to ride a horse to victory in a horse race.

Salma Hayek
Actress/Producer

Salma Hayek has been in more than 30 films. She was the first Latin to be nominated for a Best Actress Oscar. Hayek has formed her own production company. Its goal is to help Hispanic-American actors and actresses.

Salma Hayek is talented. She acts in, produces, and directs movies. But her compassion is what makes her a great human being. She campaigns against domestic violence. She gives large amounts of her own money to battered women's groups. She works to stop the spread of disease among mothers and babies.

Salma Hayek Jimenez was born on September 2, 1966, in Coatzacoalcos. This is a port city in the state of Veracruz, Mexico. Her father was in the oil business. He came to Mexico from Lebanon. Her mother was an opera singer. Her family had come to Mexico from Spain. Salma has a younger brother, Sami.

Salma's family was wealthy. She says that she and Sami were spoiled. Salma had her own horses. She also had her own private zoo. The zoo included pet tigers. Salma's mother allowed Salma's favorite tiger, Rambo, to wander about inside their house.

When Salma was 12, she went to a Catholic boarding school in Louisiana. Salma was always playing practical jokes on the nuns. One night she snuck into the nuns' dorm rooms. Salma set all the clocks back three hours. School was very late starting the next day. When Salma was caught, she was sent home!

Salma graduated from high school at 16. She enrolled at the Universidad Iberoamericana in Mexico City. She studied international relations and drama. When she was 18, she dropped out of college. She wanted a career in acting. Her parents and her friends thought she was making a big mistake.

Salma Hayek started her career by working in local theater. That gave her a chance to learn the skills she would need. She began taking roles in neighborhood theaters.

She was chosen to play the lead role of Jasmine in the children's play *Aladdin and His Marvelous Lamp.* All of the children who saw the play loved Hayek. Some of them even tried to climb up on the stage to be near her. Already it was clear that Hayek had both talent and charisma.

In 1988, Hayek was hired to play a small role on a Mexican soap opera called *A New Dawn.* The next year, Hayek won the starring role in a new soap opera called *Teresa.* This role changed Hayek's life.

Teresa became the most popular show on Mexican television. Salma Hayek became the most famous actress in Mexico. In 1989, she won two TV Novela Awards. Novela Awards are similar to the U.S. Daytime Emmy Awards. Hayek's first award was for Best Newcomer, in *A New Dawn.* The second was for Best Actress, in *Teresa.*

In 1991, Hayek decided to leave the show. She wanted to act in movies. But there was little opportunity for an actress in Mexico other than TV. Few movies were made in Mexico.

Hayek left her comfortable life in Mexico. She moved to Los Angeles. There her life became a struggle. At first, she could not drive. After she learned, she got lost all the time.

Hayek still didn't speak English. No American movie makers would hire an actress who couldn't speak the language. Finally, Hayek took 18 months off to study English. Hayek has a learning disability. As a result, she struggled to learn English.

She began to run out of money. She thought about giving up her dream and going back to Mexico. But Hayek didn't give up. She began auditioning, or trying out, for roles.

In 1993, she tried out for a role in a film called *My Crazy Life*. She auditioned over and over during a four-month period. In the end, she didn't get the part. But the director was impressed by Hayek's determination. She gave Hayek some other small parts. That way, Hayek could belong to the Screen Actors Guild. An actor who isn't part of the Guild will not be given work on most projects.

Hayek began playing small parts on various TV shows. She didn't mind that the parts were small. After all, she had to start somewhere. It upset her that she was always asked to play a Mexican female in a tight dress. Her acting ability didn't matter, just her looks.

One day in 1994, Hayek was a guest on a Spanish-language TV talk show. Hayek talked with Paul Rodriguez, the show's host. They discussed how Hispanic performers were so often asked to play stereotyped roles.

A Mexican-American film director named Robert Rodriguez (no relation to Paul) was watching the show. He was spellbound by Hayek. Rodriguez asked Hayek to play the heroine in his movie *Desperado*. The movie would also star Antonio Banderas, a Spanish actor. *Desperado* was a huge action hit in 1995.

Hollywood was still not ready for Hayek. No new roles came the way of the beautiful Mexican with the thick Spanish accent.

Hayek took her acting skills back to Mexico. In 1995, she starred in *Miracle Alley*. It won more awards than any other movie in the history of Mexican cinema. Hayek was nominated for a Silver Ariel Award (the Mexican version of the Oscar award).

Hayek returned to the United States. She went on to star in another of Rodriguez's films. In *From Dusk Till Dawn* she played a vampire. It was not an easy role. Makeup artists spent hours changing her into a vampire. She also had to do a scene in which she danced with an 11-foot python. Hayek was terrified of snakes. *From Dusk Till Dawn* became a cult favorite.

The 1997 film *Fools Rush In* was a turning point in Hayek's career. It was a romantic comedy. Hayek played a Mexican-American woman. Her character meets a young white businessman. The two fall in love. They marry within 24 hours. Afterwards, the two learn about one another in very funny ways. *Fools Rush In* was a hit.

In 1999, Hayek co-starred in Will Smith's *Wild Wild West.* For this work, she won the Blockbuster Entertainment Award for Favorite Supporting Actress. This award is voted on by the movie-going public.

Hayek branched out in other directions. In 1999, she started her own production company. She called it Ventanarosa. Literally translated, it means "rose-colored window." The company's goal was to help Hispanics have the same chances for work as other actors and actresses.

Ventanarosa's first film was *No One Writes to the Colonel* in 1999. The film was Mexico's official submission for Best Foreign Film at the Academy Awards.

In 2001, Ventanarosa produced *In the Time of Butterflies.* This film was based on a novel by Julia Alvarez.

Also in 2001, the movie *Frida* went into production. For many years, Hayek had wanted to tell the story of the artist Frida Kahlo. Kalho and her husband, Diego Rivera, are two of Mexico's most famous artists.

Frida was released in 2002. Hayek played the starring role as Frida Kahlo. For her work, she was nominated for the Best Actress Academy Award. The film itself won two Oscars.

In 2003, Hayek played her role from *Desperado* again in the film *Once Upon a Time in Mexico.* She also produced and directed *The Maldonado Miracle.* This Showtime movie earned her a Daytime Emmy for Outstanding Directing in a Family Special.

In 2006, Hayek produced an ABC TV show titled *Ugly Betty*. The show is based on a Colombian soap opera, *Yo Soy Betty La Fea*. A comedy, it tells the story of Betty Suarez. Betty is not ugly. She is average looking and has poor taste in clothing. Her job is at a fashion magazine. The show is intended to make fun of shallow people. Hayek feels strongly that women should be valued for more than their looks. *Ugly Betty* won a Golden Globe Award for Best Comedy Series in 2007.

In April 2007, Hayek and MGM announced the formation of Ventanazul. This is a film production company that focuses on Latin-themed projects. Hayek is the president and CEO of the group.

Over the years, Hayek has worked hard for many charities. One of these is the Revlon Run/Walk for breast cancer awareness. Hayek had been a model and spokesperson for the Revlon cosmetics company since 1998. Hayek worked to educate Spanish-speaking people about breast cancer.

In 2004, Hayek and the Avon Foundation formed a partnership to help end the cycle of domestic violence. The Speak Out Against Domestic Violence program includes educational material, training, and fund-raising. It also features public-service announcements. That same year, Hayek became a U.S. citizen.

In 2005, Hayek spoke to the U.S. Senate Committee on the Judiciary. She supported the Violence Against Women Act. She has also donated a great deal of her own money to a shelter for battered women in Veracruz.

Hayek became the new global spokesperson for Avon. She said, "I have a personal commitment to the cause of domestic violence. I know that by joining forces with Avon and the Avon Foundation, we can truly make a difference to the important cause of domestic violence and bring hope and empowerment to women around the world."

In September 2007, Hayek had a daughter, Valentina. Now Hayek has adopted a new cause. She has become the spokesperson for the Pampers/UNICEF program called 1 Pack = 1 Vaccine. The goal of the program is to stop the spread of tetanus in mothers and their newborn babies.

Hayek has great ambitions for her future. She says she wants to be "a much better producer. Then I want to direct again. Then I want to write. I want to have the absolute vision of what's in my head go through me, through the entire process, until I can touch it and smell it and see it." Whatever she decides to do, Salma Hayek will go after it with great passion and determination.

Remembering the Facts

1. Why was the soap opera *Teresa* important in Hayek's career?

2. Why did Hayek decide to leave Mexico?

3. How did Hayek get the lead role in *Desperado*?

4. Why was *Fools Rush In* a turning point in Hayek's career?

5. What was the goal of Hayek's production company, Ventanarosa?

6. For which role was Hayek nominated for an Oscar for Best Actress?

7. What is the message of the show *Ugly Betty*?

8. What role does Hayek fulfill for the Avon Foundation?

Understanding the Story

9. Give examples of how Salma Hayek showed determination
    in her life.

10. Why do you think Hayek's production companies are so
    important for aspiring Hispanic actors and actresses?

Getting the Main Idea

In what ways do you think Salma Hayek is a good role model for young
Americans?

Applying What You've Learned

Imagine that you are planning a career in the entertainment industry.
Write a paragraph about a job that interests you. Explain why you chose
this job. (You might choose jobs such as actor, director, photographer,
producer, special effects, stunt person, costume designer, makeup artist,
and so on.)

Christy Turlington
Supermodel

Christy Turlington is an international supermodel. She is best known for representing Calvin Klein fragrances since 1987. She has also worked with the Maybelline cosmetics company and Giorgio Armani. Christy's face is known around the world. She is a symbol of beauty and glamour.

However, Christy is not a typical model. Christy's pleasant personality makes her stand out. She is polite and professional about her work. Kurt Markus, a photographer who worked with her for years, said, "Christy's uniqueness is a combination of maintaining personal dignity and a very firm grip on manners. I have seen her tested over and over.... She is a rock."

Christy has used the money she has earned from her modeling to help others. She is a tireless worker for charities that support children, education, animal rights, and anti-tobacco campaigns.

Christy Turlington was born on January 2, 1969, in Walnut Creek, California. She was the second of three girls. Her father, Dwain, was a pilot for Pan American Airways. Her mother, Elizabeth, was a flight attendant. The couple met on a flight to Hawaii on which they were both working.

Elizabeth's family was from El Salvador, a country in Central America. They moved to the United States from El Salvador in the 1940s. Dwain's family was originally from England.

Christy grew up in Walnut Creek, a suburb of San Francisco. She and her sisters loved to play sports. Christy played soccer and ran track.

As a young girl, Christy was not happy about her looks. She often compared herself with other girls her age. Most of her friends were small and had straight light-colored hair. Christy had dark curly hair. She was always the tallest girl in the class. She felt that she did not fit in with the others. She often slouched to look shorter.

When Christy was ten, her family moved to Coral Gables, Florida. There she fell in love with horses. She took riding lessons. Then she began to ride in competitions.

One day she and her sister were at the stables for a riding lesson. Christy was spotted by a photographer named Dennie Cody. Cody took one look at 14-year-old Christy and knew she had what it took to be a model.

With their mother's permission, Cody took pictures of both girls. He asked a local modeling agency to look at the pictures. The agent said that Christy's sister was too short to be a model. But Christy might be able to find some work. Christy began modeling for local businesses after school.

In 1983, Dwain Turlington had a heart attack while jogging in the park. The airline would no longer allow him to fly planes. The family decided to move back to the San Francisco area.

In San Francisco, Christy signed with a modeling agency. She began going into the city a couple of times a week to work. She would take a bus to the train, then ride the train downtown. From there she would either walk or take a cab to the job. Christy found her work to be a lot more interesting than school. Her schoolwork suffered as a result.

Christy made up her mind to become a model. In the summer of 1984, she was 15. She and her mother went to Paris. They visited with photographers and fashion houses with little success.

The next summer, Christy went to New York. She took copies of her portfolio to magazine editors and photographers all over Manhattan. (A portfolio contains samples of a person's work—in her case, photos.) No one seemed to be interested. Christy had to go back to San Francisco. School was about to begin.

Just before she left New York, she got a call from *Vogue* magazine. They wanted to use 16-year-old Christy for some modeling jobs. Christy did go home to attend high school. But several times that year, she flew to Paris and New York on photo shoots for *Vogue*.

In 1986, the summer before her senior year, Christy moved to New York. She was now her full height of 5'10". She worked for Ford Models, a well-known modeling agency. At the end of the summer, she went home to finish high school. But the lure of modeling was too strong. By December she was back in New York.

It was exciting for Christy at first. She traveled the world. She visited many exotic places for photo shoots. The day Christy turned 18, she was on an airplane flying to Thailand. Next she did a shoot in Egypt.

When she got back to New York, she felt she was an adult. She moved into her first apartment. She kept very busy with modeling jobs. There was just one problem. She felt bad about not finishing high school. Finally, she was able to do this through an independent study school.

Designer Calvin Klein was getting ready to launch a new fragrance line called Eternity in 1987. He wanted Christy Turlington to be the "face" of the fragrance. She would be featured in all the ads for the product. She signed an exclusive contract to do ads for Eternity for the next three years. The exclusive contract meant she could only work for Klein. Magazines around the world featured photographs of her.

When her contract with Calvin Klein expired, Turlington signed a new contract with Maybelline, a cosmetics company. She made sure this five-year contract was non-exclusive. That way, she could accept other modeling jobs at the same time. However, she couldn't work for another cosmetics company.

Over the next few years, Turlington became one of the top models in the world. She was regularly featured on the cover of magazines such as *Vogue* and *Cosmopolitan*. She also did many fashion shows for famous design houses such as Chanel and Versace.

Turlington was one of three models at this time who were called "supermodels." Magazines and newspapers wrote about every detail of the trio's lives. Photographers followed them around. The photographers hoped to get some gossip or embarrassing shots.

Years later, Turlington talked about this part of her life. She said that it is very easy for a famous young model to get into bad habits. Many models become difficult and demanding. They expect everyone to treat them like royalty.

Turlington is not like that. She is known as one of the nicest models in the business. Photographer Arthur Elgort said, "Her eyes are not on the clock. She'll drive the Jeep. She'll help with the suitcases. She's never outside herself, looking at herself, saying, 'This will be good for my career.' You never hear 'Christy got in late' or 'Christy's tired.' She is worth every nickel [she is paid]."

By the time she was 26, Turlington was on top of the modeling world. But she had also realized that she didn't want to spend her life modeling. She felt that she needed new challenges in her life. She quit smoking. She began to exercise more. When she gained ten pounds, people in the fashion industry were very critical of her. Turlington said, "It led me to rethink my career. I would rather be ten pounds heavier, tobacco-free, and happy."

Turlington enrolled at New York University (NYU). She took classes on every topic that interested her. She studied philosophy, literature, art history, and religion. She later said, "It was a glorious time of personal growth. I was able to prove myself with my knowledge rather than with my body and my face."

Turlington was amazed at the reaction she got from people when she enrolled in school. Most of them laughed at her. One person even hinted that she might be able to learn how to spell! Turlington said that people often think models are worthless other than for their looks.

Turlington's father was diagnosed with lung cancer. He had never been able to follow his doctor's orders to give up smoking after his heart attack. He died on July 7, 1997. A few years later, Christy became a passionate anti-smoking activist.

Turlington earned her degree in religious studies from NYU in 1999. She was 30 years old. She decided that her next challenge would be to climb Mt. Kilimanjaro. This is the tallest peak in Africa. It is 19,340 feet tall. Turlington had seen the mountain a few years before when doing a fashion shoot in Africa.

Turlington got three friends together. They hired some guides and assistants to carry most of the gear. Still, each of the women had to carry a heavy backpack. They wore heavy boots and warm clothing.

It took them seven days to reach the summit. They battled cold weather and hailstorms. The climbing itself was grueling. Turlington later wrote, "We are breaking through ice most of the way. One wrong step and you could slide all the way back to Amsha. My feet and hands are cold, so I keep moving. It seems never ending." Once they reached the top, it took them only two days to come back down!

Turlington returned to New York. She settled into a townhouse. She had guest rooms in the townhouse for her sisters and their families as well as her mother. Turlington had earned enough from her modeling to live comfortably.

She decided to spend much of her time working with charities. She made a series of ads for People for the Ethical Treatment of Animals (PETA), an animal rights group. The ads discouraged people from killing animals to make fur clothing.

Turlington is a strong supporter of the American Cancer Society. She wanted to work for this group because of her father's death from lung cancer. She herself had been a smoker as a teenager. She found it a difficult struggle to give up the habit successfully.

Turlington's work for the American Cancer Society focuses on young women. She hopes her campaigns will discourage them from trying smoking at all. Because of her own experiences, Turlington can relate to other young women who are smokers. She has also done public service messages against smoking for Great Britain's National Health Service.

Turlington created a Web site called smokingisugly.com. The site is a resource for people who want to quit smoking. It also contains good information about lung cancer.

In the 1990s, Turlington appeared in several films about the fashion industry. *Unzipped* was a film about fashion designer Isaac Mizrahi. *Catwalk* followed Turlington and other models as they worked at major fashion shows. She also appeared in two music videos.

Turlington has appeared on more than 500 magazine covers. In 1993, her face was used on 120 mannequins! (A mannequin is a dummy human figure used to display clothing.) The mannequins were made for the Costume Institute at the Metropolitan Museum of Art. Because of this, she was called the "Face of the 20th Century."

Turlington has become a partner in three successful businesses. One is a line of skin-care products and cosmetics called Sundari. She also signed with Puma to develop both an active women's clothing line and her own line of clothing for yoga. She will not be a part of their advertising for the clothing, however.

Turlington continues to do some modeling work part-time. In 2006, she returned to Maybelline as a spokesperson. A new TV campaign targeted women older than 35. At 37, she was the perfect person for the new products.

Turlington finds much of her strength in yoga. Many of its principles are based on finding your balance as an individual. She says that finding the key to balance in your life is a key to a happy life. She says that "yoga is a practice that enables students to reach a place of deep peace, harmony, and happiness."

In 2002, Turlington wrote a book about how she has practiced yoga in her life. Its title is *Living Yoga: Creating a Life Practice*. In it, she explains how yoga has helped her through the difficult times in her life.

Turlington is chairwoman of a nonprofit group called the International Committee for Intercambios Culturales of El Salvador. The group is centered in San Salvador. Its purpose is to help rebuild the country, which is recovering from a civil war. The group has a public library and a community technology center. It also offers educational programs.

In 2003, Turlington married Ed Burns. He is an actor and filmmaker. The couple have two children, Grace and Finn. The family lives in New York City.

The lifestyle of a supermodel makes one think of parties, fame, wealth, and beauty. Few models are able to maintain balance in their lives living in such an environment. Christy Turlington did not let her self-worth be determined by her looks. Rather, she has developed herself as a person. She has found ways to use her wealth and beauty to help her fellow human beings.

Remembering the Facts

1. Why did Christy compare herself negatively with her friends as a young girl?

2. How was Christy first "discovered" for modeling?

3. Why was Christy not interested in high school?

4. What work did Turlington do for Calvin Klein?

5. How did many people react when Turlington decided to go to NYU?

6. What did Turlington do right after earning her college degree?

7. What is the goal of Turlington's work with the American Cancer Society?

8. Why does Turlington practice yoga?

Understanding the Story

9.   Why do you think it could be difficult to lead a balanced life while working as a model?

10.   Why do you think Turlington is different from many other supermodels?

Getting the Main Idea

In what ways do you think Christy Turlington is a good role model for young Americans?

Applying What You've Learned

Make an ad for a product you enjoy. Use yourself as a model in the ad. Think of a catchy slogan.

Rebecca Lobo
Basketball Player

Rebecca Lobo is a famous women's basketball player. Between 1995 and 1997, Rebecca and the teams she played on won an amazing 102 games in a row without a loss. This is the longest winning streak of any basketball player in history.

Lobo went to the University of Connecticut. She led her basketball team to the 1995 Division I NCAA championship. She won gold as a member of the U.S. Olympic women's basketball team in 1996.

Rebecca's childhood dream was to become a professional basketball player. Her dream came true when the Women's National Basketball Association (WNBA) was formed in 1996. She played for the New York Liberty, the Houston Comets, and the Connecticut Sun. An injury ended her career early. She is now a sports commentator for ESPN and CBS.

Rebecca Rose Lobo was born on October 6, 1973, in Hartford, Connecticut. Her father, Dennis Lobo, was a high-school history teacher. Her mother, RuthAnn, was a counselor. Rebecca had a sister and a brother, Rachel and Jason.

Dennis Lobo's family was half Cuban and half Polish. RuthAnn Lobo's family was German and Irish.

When Rebecca was two, the family moved to Southwick, Massachusetts. Their house had a wide driveway with a basketball hoop over the garage door. Rebecca later said, "This driveway was my

entire world while I was growing up. It had more basketballs bounced on its surface, bikes skidded over it, and skateboards ridden over its bumps than any one person can imagine."

Rebecca was just five years old when she first played basketball. Her brother, Jason, who was four years older, liked to shoot baskets. Rebecca wanted to do whatever her brother did. So she joined right in. The Lobo kids liked many sports. They were always playing something outdoors.

As early as third grade, Rebecca was very good at playing basketball. She was asked to play on a youth team. The kids on the team were five years older than she was.

Rebecca wanted to be a professional basketball player when she grew up. But there were no women's professional teams at that time. The WNBA didn't exist yet. There were only professional men's teams. Eight-year-old Rebecca sent a letter to the manager of the Celtics, Red Auerbach. She said, "I want you to know that I am going to be the first girl to play for the Boston Celtics."

In fifth grade, Rebecca played basketball with the boys at recess. A teacher suggested that Rebecca act more like a girl. Her mother was not happy. She told Rebecca that everyone has their own talents. There was nothing wrong with a girl playing basketball. So Rebecca kept playing basketball at recess. She later said her mother probably saved her career right then!

The Lobos are a tall family. Dennis is 6 feet 5 inches. RuthAnn is 5 feet 11 inches. Jason is nearly 7 feet tall. Rebecca is 6 feet 4 inches. Rachel is the shortest at "only" 5 feet 10 inches!

By the time Rebecca was in middle school, she was already 6 feet tall. She was the tallest person in her whole school. She had become very serious about basketball. She dreamed of playing professionally.

Rebecca went on to Southwick Tolland Regional High School. She played center on the school basketball team. In her first high-school game, she scored 32 points (out of the 56 scored by her entire team).

Rebecca began wearing her hair in a style that was to become her trademark. It was a long single braid. Her teammates began calling her B. "B" was short for "Becca."

Her freshman year in high school, Rebecca averaged 22.5 points per game. Her team went undefeated. She was named an AAU All-American. Rebecca was also a well-rounded student. She got excellent grades. She played the saxophone in the school band. And, in addition to basketball, she played field hockey, softball, and track.

Her sophomore year was better yet. Rebecca averaged 27 points per game. She worked hard to improve her game. If she had missed any free throws during a game, she would stay afterward to practice them.

In Rebecca's junior year, she scored 32 points per game. She was named to *Parade* magazine's All-America team. More than a hundred colleges tried to recruit Rebecca.

Rebecca's senior season was exciting. In one game, she scored 62 points! That year, she broke the state scoring record. She had scored 2,710 points during her high-school career. That was more than any other girl or boy had ever scored during the entire history of high-school basketball in Massachusetts! She was named State Player of the Year. She was a finalist for National Player of the Year.

Rebecca Lobo was recruited by the University of Connecticut Huskies. The UConn Huskies were a national power in women's basketball. Rebecca had a lot to learn about playing basketball on the college level. In her first game, she shot only 3 for 12 shots. She fouled out after just 26 minutes. But she got the hang of it fast. At the end of the season, she was named Big East Rookie of the Year.

Rebecca's sophomore year (1992–1993) was tough. Several good players had graduated. Others were injured and could not play. Most of the year, only eight players were able to play. In nearly every game, Rebecca had to play the entire time. Opposing teams would put two players on her to try to keep her from scoring. She had to work even harder to score points.

In February 1993, the Huskies played Stanford. The attendance of 8,241 at the game was a record for the Big East. The game was broadcast live on CBS. It had high ratings. This was a turning point in the popularity of women's college basketball.

Midway through Rebecca's junior year, RuthAnn Lobo told her daughter that she had breast cancer. She would need surgery and chemotherapy (drugs that treat cancer). Rebecca's mother was very ill. Still, she attended every one of her daughter's games at UConn. She said it was "kind of like (my) therapy."

Her junior year (1993–1994), Rebecca was named Big East Player of the Year. She was also named to the All-America team. When she received her trophy at the awards banquet that year, she said, "This is for my mother. She has been the real competitor this year." Then Rebecca told the press about her mother's battle with cancer. Letters of support poured in from Rebecca's fans.

In Rebecca's senior year (1994–1995), the Huskies were undefeated. They were named #1 in the country by the Associated Press poll. Rebecca was one of the most famous female athletes in the country. Young girls mobbed her after every game, seeking her autograph.

The Huskies hoped to win the National Collegiate Athletic Association (NCAA) title. They made it to the Final Four. The Huskies played the title game against Tennessee. The Huskies won the national championship 70 to 64 in front of more than 18,000 fans. Rebecca was named Most Valuable Player. What a way to end her college career!

Rebecca finished her senior year as UConn's all-time leader in blocked shots and rebounding. She got a degree in political science.

Rebecca received many honors. She was a 1995 Rhodes Scholar candidate and a NCAA top scholar athlete. She was named to the Academic All-America Team. She was also the Naismith National Player of the Year.

Rebecca Lobo still dreamed of playing basketball professionally. But her prospects were limited. The WNBA did not yet exist. She thought about a career in broadcasting. But she still wanted to play basketball. She would have to go to Europe to play on a professional team there.

In the meantime, Lobo won a spot on the U.S. national basketball team. They would play in the summer Olympic Games the next year. She was the youngest member of the team.

The team worked hard to prepare for the Olympics. First they went on a 20-game national tour in the United States. They played the best college teams. Then they took a world tour, playing the best teams in Europe. At the end of the tour, they had a record of 52–0. They had won every game.

The 1996 Summer Olympic Games were held in Atlanta, Georgia. The U.S. women's team far outplayed all their opponents. They won every game to cinch the gold medal! After the win, Lobo met President Bill Clinton at the White House. He invited her to go jogging with him.

In 1996, Rebecca and RuthAnn Lobo wrote a mother-daughter autobiography. It was called *The Home Team*. In the book, they told the story of their lives and RuthAnn's battle with cancer.

Lobo also talked about how sports had helped her work through the problems she had while growing up. The physical workout of a game always helped her forget her troubles. She said, "Most people need some way to handle the pain or anxiety in their lives. Basketball became my way."

Lobo's basketball career had created a lot of interest in women's professional basketball. The National Basketball Association (NBA) decided to help form a league for women, the WNBA. The new league would be supported by the NBA until it got going on its own. The WNBA began playing in the summer of 1997.

Lobo was assigned to the New York Liberty. The Liberty was one of eight charter teams. Her first contract was for $250,000. Lobo's dream had come true. She had become a professional basketball player.

Lobo also signed endorsement contracts. Reebok named a shoe for her: The Lobo. (Rebecca Lobo wore a size 12 shoe!)

Lobo became a spokesperson for the WNBA. She was already so popular with fans that she was a natural choice. The vice president of the Liberty, Carol Blazejowski, said, "Rebecca Lobo has done more for women's basketball in the region and in the nation than anybody." Lobo became known as "the ambassador of women's basketball."

The WNBA games were broadcast on three networks: ESPN, NBC, and Lifetime. The attendance at the Liberty's games the first year averaged more than 13,000 people. Many people came because they wanted to see Rebecca Lobo play.

It was a big adjustment playing in the WNBA. Lobo was one of the youngest players. Still, she led her team in rebounds in both 1997 and 1998. She was second in scoring both years. And the fans loved her. Jerseys with her name on them were among the top-selling items in the league.

In the 1999 season opener, disaster struck. After playing only one minute, Lobo suffered a terrible knee injury. She had to have surgery to repair a torn ligament. Six months later, Lobo injured the same knee again. The surgery had to be repeated. Lobo ended up being out for the entire 1999 and 2000 seasons.

Lobo worked hard to recover from her injury. She said, "My goals have gone from being an all-star to just being able to play basketball. I always took for granted that I could play. Now I know what a gift it is."

Lobo returned to the Liberty lineup in 2001. After playing 16 games, she was traded to the Houston Comets in 2002. She finished her career with the Connecticut Sun in 2003. She had never fully recovered from the injuries to her knee.

Rebecca Lobo married Steve Rushin in 2003. He was a writer for *Sports Illustrated.* Later, the couple had two daughters.

Today, Lobo provides analysis of women's college and WNBA games for ESPN, CBS, and other networks. She is also a very popular motivational speaker.

Rebecca Lobo is an active supporter of charities that deal with children, breast cancer, and education. She and her mother have set up the RuthAnn and Rebecca Lobo Scholarship in Allied Health. The scholarship is awarded yearly. It goes to a student who plans to enroll in the School of Allied Health, now the Department of Allied Health Sciences, at the University of Connecticut. The two have taken part in many other events to raise money for breast cancer research.

Rebecca Lobo knows she is a role model for young women. She takes this responsibility seriously. She said, "I think athletes have a responsibility to realize that little eyes are watching them. I want to be a good person and live my life the right way, keeping in mind that there might be a little kid who's watching what I do."

She often speaks at schools. She tells the students, "Be a good person and study hard. Don't do drugs. Treat other people, no matter who they are, with respect and dignity and fairness. Remember that even if opportunities aren't there now, that doesn't mean they won't be there next year or five years from now. Have goals and dreams. I've had so many dreams come true in my life."

Remembering the Facts

1. Why was Rebecca's childhood dream of playing pro basketball not realistic at the time?

2. What was Rebecca's trademark?

3. What scoring record did Rebecca break in her high-school career?

4. What illness did RuthAnn Lobo have during Rebecca's junior year in college?

5. How did the UConn Huskies do during the 1995 NCAA basketball tournament?

6. What did Lobo do during the summer after she graduated from college?

7. Why was Lobo chosen as a spokesperson for the WNBA?

8. Why did Lobo have to retire from basketball in 2003?

Understanding the Story

9. Why do you think Rebecca Lobo was an important factor in the decision to form the WNBA in 1996?

10. Why do you think Rebecca Lobo chooses to support charities that deal with children, breast cancer, and education?

Getting the Main Idea

In what ways do you think Rebecca Lobo is a good role model for young Americans?

Applying What You've Learned

Make a list of products you think would be appropriate for a professional basketball player to endorse. Choose one of these products. Make a poster showing a current basketball player endorsing the product you chose.

16 MORE **Extraordinary** Hispanic Americans

Alex Rodriguez
Baseball Player

Alex Rodriguez (nicknamed A-Rod) is one of the best players in baseball. He has been the third baseman for the New York Yankees since 2004. Before that, he played shortstop for the Seattle Mariners and the Texas Rangers. Rodriguez uses his wealth and fame to help others.

Rodriguez is the youngest player ever to hit 500 home runs. He is the highest-paid player in baseball. In 2007, he signed a $275 million contract with the New York Yankees.

Alex Rodriguez was born on July 27, 1975, in New York City. He has an older brother and sister named Joe and Susy.

Alex's parents are Victor and Lourdes Rodriguez. They are both from the Dominican Republic. This is a country on an island in the Caribbean Sea. The couple loved it there. But it was very hard to make a living. The average wage was less than $1,000 a year.

They moved to New York City soon after their marriage. Victor opened a shoe store. He worked long hours. As a toddler, Alex ran up and down the store's aisles swinging a huge red plastic bat.

The store did well. By the time Alex was four years old, Victor had made enough money for the family to return to the Dominican Republic.

Baseball is the major sport in the Dominican Republic. Because of the warm climate, the game is played year-round. Alex played baseball every minute he wasn't in school. Victor had once been a catcher in the Domincan professional baseball league. He practiced with young Alex.

When Alex was eight, Victor needed to go back to work. He moved his family to Miami. He opened a new shoe store.

When Alex was nine, his father left home. He never came back. Alex's mother had to support the family. She worked in an office during the day. At night, she waitressed. Susy and Joe took care of Alex.

When Alex was 11, he joined a baseball team at the Boys & Girls Club of Miami. The club offered after-school programs and sports. Alex's baseball coach was Eddie Rodriguez. (He had no relation to Alex.)

Eddie spent a lot of time with Alex. He told him of the great players he had coached at the Boys & Girls Club. These included Jose Canseco, Alex Fernandez, and Rafael Palmeiro. All of them were now major-league players. Eddie told Alex he could be a major-league player, too, if he worked hard.

Alex had a second adult male role model. He was Juan Arteaga, the father of Alex's friend J. D. Arteaga. Juan Arteaga treated Alex as his own son. He bought the boys gloves and drove them to their games.

Alex and J.D. went to high school at Westminster Christian High School. It was a small private school. The school demanded the best from students. Westminster also had a great sports program. Its baseball team was one of the best in the United States.

Alex and J.D. played baseball, football, and basketball together. Juan Arteaga was always there to watch. But he had a heart attack and died at one of their games. Alex later said, "Everything he gave to his son, he gave to me. I still play in his honor."

At the beginning of his tenth-grade season, Alex was tall and skinny. He did not make the starting lineup on the baseball team. His friend J.D. was the star pitcher. Alex worked hard to improve.

Alex was a well-rounded student and athlete. He was quarterback for the school football team. He played point guard on the basketball team. He studied hard. He was an honor-roll student.

When baseball practice began in Alex's junior year, Alex was 6'2" and 185 pounds. He had gained 2 inches in height and 30 pounds of muscle. He was faster and stronger than the year before. This time, Alex was one of the top players on the team.

That year, *USA Today* named Westminster the number-one high-school baseball team in the country. Alex and eight teammates were named to the Florida all-state team. Alex and one teammate were high-school All-Americans.

At the age of 16, Alex was already what baseball scouts call a five-tool player. He excelled at all the skills a good player should have. These are throwing, hitting for a high average, fielding, running, and hitting with power. Not many players in baseball are five-tool players.

When Alex began his senior baseball season, *Baseball America* named him the top high-school prospect in the country. At his first game, 62 scouts were in the stands. Alex was under a lot of pressure. But he didn't let it affect how he played. He ended the year with a .505 batting average. He had 9 home runs, 36 RBIs, and 35 stolen bases.

The major-league draft was held on June 3, 1993. Alex, his friends and family, and many reporters waited for the results at a party at J.D.'s house. At 1:14 P.M., 17-year-old Alex learned that he was the number-one draft pick in the country! He had been chosen by the Seattle Mariners. (J.D. was picked by the New York Mets in the fifth round.)

Alex didn't sign with the Mariners right away. He had a choice to make. He had also received a baseball scholarship to the University of Miami. If the Mariners didn't offer him enough money, he planned to play college baseball. He would be eligible for the draft again after his junior year.

Alex and the Mariners negotiated all summer. Alex wanted a million-dollar contract. The Mariners didn't want to pay that much. But time was running out. Once Alex started attending classes, the Mariners could no longer sign him. Just two hours before Alex was to attend his first class, the two sides came to an agreement. Alex's contract would be $1.3 million. It was the most ever paid to a player right out of high school.

Alex didn't let the money go to his head. He bought a new car. He kept $1,000 a month to live on. Then he paid off the mortgage on his mother's house. He bought her a new car. He saved the rest of the money. He was thankful for all the years his mom had worked so hard to support him.

Most new players spend their first years with a minor-league team. Alex Rodriguez went to the Mariner's Single-A team, the Appleton Foxes, in Wisconsin.

But it soon became clear that Single-A ball was too easy for Rodriguez. So the Mariners sent him up to their Double-A team in Jacksonville, Florida. For most players, this is a big leap. Rodriguez played just as well in Double-A baseball.

In 1994, the Mariners had a chance to win their division. But they needed a spark to get them going. Manager Lou Piniella had seen Rodriguez play. He thought Rodriguez could be the spark the team needed. So, on July 8, 1994, Rodriguez was called up to the majors. He was 18 years old and just a year out of high school.

Rodriguez flew to Boston. The Mariners were going to play the Red Sox in Fenway Park. He was in the starting lineup as shortstop. In his second game against Boston, Alex Rodriguez got his first hit in the major leagues!

After the end of the season, Rodriguez was ready to play more baseball. The Mariners asked him to play winter-league baseball. Winter league is played in the warm countries of the Caribbean.

Rodriguez played for a team in the Dominican Republic. He enjoyed being there. He had forgotten much about the country. He had lived in the States so long that his Spanish was rusty, too.

In 1995, the Mariners decided Rodriguez should start the season with their Triple-A team in Tacoma, Washington. Over the season, he was sent back and forth between the Triple-A team and the majors. He was frustrated. He kept working hard trying to improve his skills.

At the end of the season, Rodriguez returned to Miami for a break. He didn't rest. He began working out with a trainer six days a week. He also worked on his diet. He was determined to be in the best shape he could when the 1996 season began.

It worked. Alex Rodriguez was named starting shortstop for the Mariners for the 1996 season. Lou Piniella put him at number two in the batting order, right in front of Ken Griffey Jr.

Rodriguez was the youngest player in the American League. He was given the nickname A-Rod. Two days before his 21st birthday, the Mariners gave him a $10 million, four-year contract.

Rodriguez did not let his fame go to his head. He said, "My mother taught me to be respectful of others, save my money, and stay humble." He is easy-going and well-mannered. Because of this, he is well-liked.

In the 1996 season, Rodriguez led the American League in hitting. He had a .358 batting average. He led the league in runs scored, total bases, and doubles. He had 36 home runs and 123 runs batted in (RBIs). He won the Silver Slugger award as the best-hitting shortstop in the league. (He would win this honor nearly every year after this.)

When the season ended, Rodriguez was named to a major-league all-star team. They played exhibition games in Japan. Cal Ripken was on the same team. He had been Rodriguez's boyhood hero. The two became friends. Rodriguez said, "I learned from Cal to respect the game, respect the fans. Nothing fancy out there. Just do your job."

Rodriguez's second year (1997) was not as productive. Still, he had 23 home runs and 84 RBIs. He did something most players never do. He hit what is called "the cycle." That means he hit a single, double, triple, and home run all in the same game!

In 1998, Rodriguez had a great season. He joined the "40-40 Club." That meant he had at least 40 home runs and 40 stolen bases in the same year. Only two other players had ever done this in the history of baseball! He was named the American League Player of the Year.

In 1999, Rodriguez missed more than 30 games due to a knee injury. Still, he hit 42 home runs that season.

In 2000, his contract with the Mariners expired. Rodriguez became a free agent. The question was, who would sign him next? There was no question that his contract would be huge. In the end, the Texas Rangers signed him to a ten-year contract worth $252 million. It was the biggest contract in sports history.

Rodriguez's 2001 and 2002 seasons broke many records. He hit 52 home runs in 2001 and had 135 RBIs. In 2002, he had 57 home runs. He won a Gold Glove award for outstanding defense. At the age of 27, he was called the best player in baseball.

In 2002, Rodriguez married Cynthia Scurtis. They later divorced in 2008. The couple had two daughters together.

In 2003, Rodriguez led the American League in home runs and runs scored. He won his second Gold Glove award. He became the youngest player to hit 300 home runs. He also won his first American League MVP (Most Valuable Player) award.

In 2004, Rodriguez was traded to the New York Yankees. Derek Jeter was already the shortstop. A-Rod became the third baseman.

In 2005, he won his second American League MVP award. He hit 48 home runs that year. In 2006, he pounded out his 450th home run and his 2,000th hit on the same swing!

On August 4, 2007, Rodriguez hit his 500th career home run. At the age of 32, he was the youngest player ever to do this. That same year, he won the Players Choice Award for Player of the Year. He also was named MVP for the American League for the third time in his career.

Rodriguez has said that he'd like to remain a Yankee for the rest of his career. On November 15, 2007, he signed a ten-year contract for $275 million. If he breaks the all-time home-run record during this time, he will get millions more.

Rodriguez has used his fame and fortune to help others. He remembers what the Boys & Girls Club of Miami did for him as a child. He says, "The streets were there, but, for my sake, so was the Boys & Girls Club." For years, Rodriguez has supported his childhood club with his time and money. Since 2002, he has been one of three national spokespersons for the Boys & Girls Clubs of America (BGCA). He pledged $500,000 to build an educational center at the BGCA in Miami.

Rodriguez also supports the University of Miami. In 2002, he donated $3.9 million to the school to remodel the baseball stadium. It will be renamed Alex Rodriguez Park. He funded a four-year scholarship to the university. Every year, a graduate of the Boys & Girls Club of Miami will be chosen as the winner.

In 2005, Rodriguez donated money to fully fund five day-care centers in the Dominican Republic. He supplied all their needs for a year.

In 2006, Rodriguez and his family set up the AROD Family Foundation. Its purpose is to help troubled families. It will do this by supporting programs "focusing on improving quality of life, education, and mental health."

Rodriguez has also written two children's books. *Hit a Grand Slam* (1998) is the story of his life. It encourages children to follow their dreams, even if the going gets rough. *Out of the Ballpark* (2007) is the story of a young boy who achieves his dreams through hard work.

Rodriguez is one of the finest baseball players in the game. He is also a fine person. Texas Rangers manager Jerry Narron once said of him, "He is without a doubt the best player in baseball, but that's not what impresses me most. I only hope that someday he might be as good a player as he is a person."

Remembering the Facts

1. How did the Boys & Girls Club of Miami help Alex when he was young?

2. How did Juan Arteaga help Alex?

3. Why was Westminster a good place for Alex to play baseball in high school?

4. At what point in his life was Alex Rodriguez first called up to the major leagues?

5. Why is baseball so popular in the Domincan Republic?

6. In what three years did Rodriguez win the American League Most Valuable Player award?

7. How has Rodriguez supported the Boys & Girls Club of Miami?

8. What two things has Rodriguez done to support the University of Miami?

Understanding the Story

9. Which people do you think were good examples to Rodriguez when he was growing up?

10 What do you think might be some reasons a young player might choose to play professional sports rather than go to college?

Getting the Main Idea

In what ways do you think Alex Rodriguez is a good role model for young Americans?

Applying What You've Learned

Make a list of words that you think best describe Alex Rodriguez.

Scott Gomez
Hockey Player

Scott Gomez is the first Hispanic-American National Hockey League (NHL) player. Gomez was named NHL Rookie of the Year in 2000. He has been an NHL All-Star. His team has won the Stanley Cup twice. He represented the United States in the 2006 Winter Olympic Games. And he did all that before his 30th birthday!

Scott Carlos Gomez was born on December 23, 1979, in Anchorage, Alaska. Scott's father, Carlos Gomez, was the son of migrant Mexican farm workers. Every year, Carlos's family traveled north from Mexico to pick crops in the United States.

Carlos Gomez was born in California. This made him a U.S. citizen. He lived with an aunt in San Diego so he could go to U.S. schools. When he graduated from high school, Carlos went to Alaska. He had a job as an iron worker on the Alaskan fuel pipeline.

Scott's mother, Dalia, was born in Colombia, South America. When she was five, she and her father went to live with family in New York. Later, they moved to Alaska.

Carlos and Dalia met in Anchorage and got married. They later had three children, Monica, Scott, and Natalie.

Carlos Gomez bought Scott his first pair of hockey skates when he was four years old. At first, Scott didn't like hockey. His friends had already started playing hockey and could skate well. Scott said, "I couldn't skate. I was afraid the other kids would make fun of me.

16 MORE Extraordinary Hispanic Americans

I wanted to quit. I told my mom I was going to get hurt, that it was too rough." Carlos wouldn't let Scott quit that easily.

Scott was a quick learner. It was clear he had potential. So Carlos took Scott to see a "real" hockey game at the University of Alaska when he was five. Scott loved what he saw.

Scott began watching a lot of hockey games on TV. He copied what he saw the hockey players doing. He began to understand what it took to be a good player.

Scott began playing in a youth hockey league sponsored by the Boys & Girls Club of Anchorage. By the time he was 12, he was playing Midget hockey for the Alaska Allstars. This was the most advanced level of Alaskan youth hockey.

By this time, Scott was very focused on hockey. He got up early nearly every day to practice. He got to the skating rink before the sun rose so it would be empty. Scott worked really hard.

Scott had "good instincts." He knew where each player was on the ice. He could tell what each was going to do next. Because of this, he could pass the puck just to the right spot. He was also skilled at scoring goals.

Scott played hockey on his high-school team. In his 10th-grade year, the team won the state championship. Scott was named Player of the Year for his 10th- and 11th-grade years. He dominated Alaskan high-school hockey.

Playing all this hockey was expensive. Carlos and Dalia Gomez raised money for Scott and his teams. Carlos organized raffles and pizza sales. The couple even had a taco booth at the Alaska State Fair.

When Scott turned 16, he left Alaska to play in the British Columbia Junior Hockey League in Canada. He played for the South Surrey Eagles in Surrey, Canada. He lived with a host family in nearby Vancouver. Scott missed his family. He spent $1,800 calling home that year!

For the first time, Scott encountered racism. Opposing players made fun of him because he was Hispanic. He was often called horrible names. It hurt his feelings. Scott learned to ignore these remarks. He realized that many were made out of ignorance. Many were made by players who were the worst in the league.

Scott proved himself on the ice. He was named the team's Most Valuable Player. He was also Rookie of the Year in the league. The South Surrey Eagles won the Western Canadian Championship in 1997 with Scott's help.

After Scott finished high school, several colleges offered him hockey scholarships. Scott decided on Colorado College. But then he changed his mind. He moved to Kennewick, Washington.

In Kennewick, Scott played the 1997–1998 season for the Tri-City Americans. This was a junior team in the Western Hockey League (WHL). Many promising young men played in the WHL. It was considered a stepping-stone to the National Hockey League (NHL).

For the first time in his career, Scott had a bad year. He injured his shoulder. He couldn't play up to his usual standards. It was not until the second half of the season that he began to feel better. During that year, Scott learned a lot about working hard to overcome adversity.

The NHL draft was near. The draft is a yearly event in which teams get to pick the new young players they want on their team.

The New Jersey Devils thought that Scott Gomez was their kind of player. The Devils played a smart, thinking game of hockey. They turned the other teams' mistakes into points for their team. The Devils thought Gomez would fit right in. They thought he played much like Wayne Gretzky. Gretzky has been called the greatest hockey player of all time.

When the draft was held, Gomez went in the first round! He was chosen 27th by the New Jersey Devils. He was only 19 years old.

Not long after the draft, Gomez arrived at the Devils' training camp. He knew he would not be actually playing for the Devils that year. First-year players usually are sent to the minor leagues. They must get more experience before they move up. The Devils wanted Gomez to see what the big-league camp would be like. They soon saw how skilled he was.

After camp, Scott Gomez was sent back to the WHL. He had a great season. He scored 30 goals and 78 assists in just 58 games! (An assist means that a player passes the puck to another player who is in position to make a goal.)

The Devils had Gomez come to New Jersey to train with Vladimir Bure. Bure was a former Russian Olympian. He was an expert at getting young hockey players into shape for the NHL. Scott later described his training under Bure as "the toughest thing I had ever been through."

By the time the Devils' training camp opened, Gomez was in great shape. He hoped he would make the Devils' lineup for the fall season.

Coach Robbie Ftorek liked what he saw in Gomez. He was quick and strong. His passing was accurate. Gomez also had the unusual skill of knowing what other players were going to do next. Gomez played hard in training camp. He told himself that he was going to make the Devils take him.

The timing was right for Gomez. Three Devils players were having contract disputes with the team. During this time, they were off the ice. Because of this, Gomez got plenty of ice time in camp. It became clear that he was not only skilled. He also had a great understanding of the game. He had another important quality. Scott Gomez was a leader. His teammates played better when he was on the ice.

At the end of the training camp, Gomez made the cut. He was given a jersey with the number 23 on it. Gomez was on the team for the 1999–2000 season.

As the first Hispanic American in the NHL, Scott Gomez began getting a lot of attention. Many people of Hispanic origin live in the New York/New Jersey area. All the major area newspapers ran stories about him. Gomez thought the stories were funny. Many exaggerated his life story. He said, "They make it sound like I crossed the border two years ago."

Gomez began pulling his weight on the team right away. On December 26, 1999, the Devils were playing their rivals, the New York Rangers. Gomez scored all three goals in the game. This was three days after his 20th birthday. He was the youngest Devil ever to score a hat trick (three goals in one game).

Gomez's opponents thought they could intimidate him because of his youth. But he let them know he could handle the pressure. Soon they backed off. Gomez kept on going. He was the only Devil to play in every one of the team's 82 games in the 1999–2000 season. He scored 19 goals and 51 assists for a total of 70 points. This was a new team record for a rookie.

Gomez was helping the Devils in another way. He was having the time of his life playing in the NHL. Some of the older players began to improve their attitudes. They remembered that playing hockey was fun!

In January 2000, Gomez was the leading scorer of all NHL rookies. Because of this, he was chosen to play in the NHL All-Star Game. He was the only rookie playing on the North American team. He was thrilled to line up with some of the greatest names in hockey.

Playoff time rolled around. The Devils made it to the finals. They faced the Dallas Stars, who had won the Stanley Cup the year before. The Devils were considered the underdogs against the tough Dallas team.

The Stanley Cup is won by the top NHL team. To win, a team must win four out of up to seven possible games against the opposing team. In 2000, the New Jersey Devils won the Cup in six games. Gomez scored four goals and six assists for a total of ten points.

Gomez was chosen by his fellow hockey players as the top first-year player in the NHL. He also won the Calder Memorial Trophy as the NHL Rookie of the Year.

After winning the Stanley Cup, each member of the Devils team got to have the Cup for a few days. Gomez took the Cup home to Alaska. He took it to a hospital to show to the sick children. He took it to a retirement home. Then he took it to downtown Anchorage on a dog sled. (A dog sled is a traditional way to travel in areas that have a great deal of ice and snow.) More than 8,000 fans were waiting to see him.

Instead of a parade, Gomez was honored with a blanket toss. This is a tradition of Native Americans in Alaska. A group threw him 20 feet into the air on a giant blanket made of sealskin (and caught him).

Gomez returned to New Jersey for the 2000–2001 hockey season. At 21, he was now a veteran player. This season, he scored 63 points. The Devils made it to the Stanley Cup finals again. The Colorado Avalanche defeated them in seven games.

The 2001–2002 season was disappointing for Gomez. He scored only 48 points. He missed the playoffs due to an injury.

The 2002–2003 season was better. Gomez scored 55 points. He helped the New Jersey Devils win the Stanley Cup again. He scored 12 points during the playoffs.

Gomez scored 70 points in the 2003–2004 season. That year he tied for the NHL lead in assists with a total of 56.

In 2004–2005, there was a dispute between the NHL and the NHL players' association. The NHL ended up canceling the entire hockey season. Gomez went home to Anchorage. He played for the Alaska Aces for the season. The Aces are part of the ECHL. (This was formerly known as the East Coast Hockey League.) He led the ECHL in scoring. He won the Most Valuable Player award even though his season was cut short by a broken pelvis.

Gomez had his best season so far in 2005–2006. He scored 84 points (33 goals and 51 assists) in 82 games. He scored another 60 points in the 2006–2007 season.

On July 1, 2007, Scott Gomez signed a seven-year, $51.5 million contract with the New York Rangers. In his first season with the Rangers, he scored 70 points.

On February 1, 2008, Gomez scored his 500th career point. During the 2008 playoff games, an announcer called him "one of the best players on the ice."

Scott Gomez has represented the United States in international competition, too. In 2004, he was part of the Ice Hockey World Championships in Prague, Czech Republic. Then in 2006, he competed in the Winter Olympic Games in Torino, Italy.

Gomez has opened the door for greater diversity in hockey. More and more Hispanic youngsters are signing up for youth leagues. Gomez has become a role model for these young players. Hispanic adults are becoming more interested in the sport.

The NHL would like to be more diverse. Nearly all its players are white. Scott Gomez was asked to work on the NHL's Diversity Task Force. This program seeks to interest kids from various backgrounds in playing hockey.

Gomez has used his fame to help others less fortunate than himself. He started the Scotty Gomez Foundation. Its purpose is to support youth hockey in Alaska. It seeks to help kids who can't afford to play hockey. It gives them money to buy equipment and other needs. The foundation has built a new hockey rink at a school in Anchorage.

Hispanic Magazine said this about Scott Gomez in 2007: "He entered the league as a rookie. In less than a year, he became an icon and a promise for the future of American hockey. Today Gomez is an established professional.... He's more than a great hockey player. He is a real-life example that hard work and dedication lead to greatness."

Remembering the Facts

1. Where did Scott Gomez grow up?

2. How did Scott's parents raise money to pay for him to play hockey?

3. What NHL team drafted Gomez in the first round?

4. What is a hat trick?

5. In what years did Gomez and the New Jersey Devils win the Stanley Cup?

6. Why did Gomez play for the Alaska Aces for the 2004–2005 season?

7. What milestone did Gomez celebrate on February 1, 2008?

8. What is the purpose of the Scotty Gomez Foundation?

Understanding the Story

9.   Why do you think the NHL would like to have more diversity among its players?

10.   Why do you think it might be unusual for Hispanic Americans to play ice hockey?

Getting the Main Idea

In what ways do you think Scott Gomez is a good role model for young Americans?

Applying What You've Learned

Write a paragraph explaining what characteristics you think a person would need to be a successful ice-hockey player.

Vocabulary

Franklin Chang-Díaz

space shuttle	plasma	propulsion	descent
scholarship	fusion	naturalized	astrophysics
deploy	tethered	cosmonaut	payload

Joseph Unanue

sardines	mechanical engineering	export
bodega	strategy	complex
distributor	institute	honorary doctorate

Guy Gabaldon

Saipan	suicide	surrender	citation
pillbox	hostile	military	civilian
descent	internment camp	interpreter	invasion
brig	reprimand	court martial	Pied Piper
samurai	barrio		

Nicholasa Mohr

illustrator	bilingual	hostile	sweatshop
trade school	academic	seamstress	graffiti
stimulating	optimism	adaptation	honorary doctorate

Isabel Allende

magical realism	novelist	diplomat	machismo
feminist	radical	socialist	economy
coup	coma	unconscious	foundation
honorary doctorate	sepia	trilogy	alleviate

 MORE Extraordinary Hispanic Americans

Mario Molina

chlorofluorocarbons	CFCs	ozone
chemical engineering	catastrophic	physical chemistry
chemical laser	post-doctoral	chlorine
propellant	atmosphere	(UV) rays
atmoshpere	protocol	fossil fuel emissions
atmospheric chemistry		

Bill Richardson

politician	political science	fraternity	international affairs
bilingual	campaign	diplomat	negotiate
intern	biofuel	nominee	privileged
hostage	Cabinet	ambassador	recession
nominate			

Carlos Santana

generation	Grammy	congas	timbales
humanitarian	foundation	mariachi	platinum
fusion	guru	meditation	vegetarian

Antonia Hernandez

counsel	tamale	picket line	discriminate
legal aid	judiciary	immigration	bilingual
nomination	proposition	advocate	controversial
contribution	foundation	potential	interdependent
integration	mobility		

Gloria Estefan

Grammy	communist	refugee	communications
psychology	vertebra	fused	platinum
congressional	inducted	foundation	royalties

Edgar Prado

jockey	communicate	thoroughbred	hand
endurance	anticipation	laminitis	devastated
compassion	exemplify	scholarship	

Salma Hayek

compassion	domestic violence	charisma	soap opera
audition	learning disability	determination	stereotype
python	production	foundation	tetanus
ambition			

Christy Turlington

supermodel	fragrance	cosmetics	stewardess
competition	portfolio	exotic	exclusive
diagnose	passionate	grueling	ethical
mannequin	yoga	harmony	

Rebecca Lobo

Olympic	professional	commentator	trademark
undefeated	broadcast	chemotherapy	autograph
autobiography	charter	endorsement	ambassador
motivational	scholarship		

Alex Rodriguez

professional	major league	negotiated	exhibition
free agent	scholarship	foundation	

Scott Gomez

league	rookie	Stanley Cup	Olympic
migrant	potential	dominate	racism
scholarship	adversity	accurate	hat trick
intimidate	champagne	pelvis	competition
diversity	foundation	icon	professional

16 MORE Extraordinary Hispanic Americans

Answer Key

Franklin Chang-Díaz

Remembering the Facts

1. the launch of the satellite *Sputnik*

2. He got a job as a research assistant in the physics lab.

3. He wanted to experience zero gravity. He wanted to look out the window of the spacecraft at Earth.

4. Mir was a Soviet space station.

5. He deployed *Galileo,* which would explore Jupiter.

6. He tied the record for the most flights in space by an astronaut.

7. AARC stands for Ad Astra Rocket Company. It is Chang-Díaz's company. Its mission is the development of a new kind of rocket technology called VASIMR.

8. It is much faster than traditional rocket engines. It will enable spaceships to carry much larger payloads (more cargo).

Understanding the Story

Answers will vary. Sample answers:

9. The loss of his four-year scholarship could have been devastating. But Franklin took the opportunity of working in the physics lab and turned it to his advantage. By hard work, he was able to complete his education and gain good experience at the same time. Franklin felt he had achieved the American dream.

10. He is a hero because he is one of Costa Rica's most famous native sons. He had to leave Costa Rica to achieve his dreams. But he did not forget where he came from. He has recruited international students to work in his lab. He has also supported space programs in Latin America.

Getting the Main Idea

Answers will vary. Sample answer:
Franklin Chang-Díaz worked hard to achieve his goals, even though they often appeared to be impossible to achieve.

Applying What You've Learned

Answers will vary.

Joseph Unanue

Remembering the Facts

1. He was homesick for the tastes and cooking of his native land.

2. He thought Goya was easier to pronounce than his own name.

3. They were sold in bodegas, small local grocery stores.

4. Cubans and Dominicans

5. Mexican Americans were already loyal to existing companies that sold Mexican products.

6. Goya employees deliver the products directly to the stores. They talk to the store managers/owners and find out what foods their customers are asking for.

7. Goya supports events in the Hispanic community such as music events, sports teams, parades, beauty contests, and festivals.

8. The institute sponsors a variety of Hispanic programs. It oversees a major in Latino studies at the university.

Understanding the Story

Answers will vary. Sample answers:

9. People from over 20 different countries are classified as Hispanic Americans. The countries are located in Central America, South America, Mexico, Spain, and the Caribbean. Because of geographic and cultural diversity, they have different food preferences as well.

10. Different groups of Hispanic Americans arrived in the United States at different times

and for different reasons. As each group arrived, Goya Foods added new foods to its product line to meet their needs. As the population of Hispanic Americans grew, so did the Goya company.

Getting the Main Idea

Answers will vary. Sample answer:
Joseph Unanue is a good role model because he worked hard to reach his goal of meeting the needs of the diverse Hispanic-American population. He has given back to his roots by furthering Hispanic culture and studies. He has also been generous with those in need.

Applying What You've Learned

Answers will vary.

Guy Gabaldon

Remembering the Facts

1. Two of his best friends were Japanese. They taught him some phrases. He went to language school with them. He lived with their family.

2. The United States entered World War II. Guy's Japanese friends were sent away to an internment camp.

3. Saipan was needed as an air base. It was within flight distance from Japan for U.S. bombers.

4. The Japanese troops were dug into the hills in caves.

5. He spoke to them in Japanese. He convinced them that they would be treated humanely and given food and medical care.

6. He brought in prisoners who had useful information. Knowing what the Japanese would do next saved lives.

7. They had heard that troops roasted and ate children.

8. *Hell to Eternity*

Understanding the Story

Answers will vary. Sample answers:

9. He gained compassion and understanding of people of other ethnic backgrounds. He learned to speak Japanese well enough to communicate.

10. Gabaldon's story was unusual and impressive. His actions showed heroism and compassion.

Getting the Main Idea

Answers will vary. Sample answer:
He was an important factor in the U.S. victory in the Battle of Saipan. His actions resulted in fewer casualties than might have occurred otherwise.

Applying What You've Learned

Paragraphs will vary.

Nicholasa Mohr

Remembering the Facts

1. She writes about the life of Puerto Ricans in New York City.

2. It has been a way to help face difficulties and make problems seem lighter.

3. She began drawing pictures and writing letters. She found that she could create her own world.

4. She insisted that a Puerto Rican girl had no need for academic education. She sent Nicholasa to a trade high school.

5. She wanted to study the works of the great Mexican painters such as Frida Kahlo, Deigo Rivera, and José Clemente Orozco.

6. She says her work was full of bold figures, faces, and various symbols of the city. The symbols were numbers, letters, words, and phrases—a kind of graffiti.

7. It is about a girl named Nilda growing up in El Barrio in New York City. She finds that drawing pictures and writing stories helps her face poverty and prejudice.

8. At that time, there were no books about Puerto Rican children growing up.

Understanding the Story

Answers will vary. Sample answers:

9. She created her own world. By drawing and painting, she could escape to a magic world that she created.

10. Both art and writing seek to convey feelings and emotions. Both may tell a story. Both can share information. Both can allow a person to imagine what another place might be like.

Getting the Main Idea

Answers will vary. Sample answer:

Nicholasa Mohr didn't let low expectations and prejudice get in her way. She worked hard and followed her dreams. She was able to have an important impact in the fields of art and literature.

Applying What You've Learned

Answers will vary.

Isabel Allende

Remembering the Facts

1. It is weaving together real and imaginary events to form a story.

2. After her grandmother's death, she found reading as an escape from her sadness.

3. She told her children many old family stories in the evenings.

4. Her grandfather believed in machismo, the idea that women are weak and inferior to men. Isabel believed in feminism, the idea that women and men are equal.

5. Her cousin Salvador Allende had been killed in a coup. His supporters were being killed, put in prison, or simply made to disappear. Isabel was working to help those who were in danger. By doing so, she put herself and her family in danger.

6. She could not come to see him, as she was in exile. So she wrote him a long letter full of family stories that she later made into a book.

7. Allende's daughter Paula was in a coma. Allende sat at Paula's bedside telling Paula family stories and the story of her own life. Allende wrote down these stories and published them as the book *Paula*.

8. The foundation supports groups that help women and children in the areas of health, education, and other needs.

Understanding the Story

Answers will vary. Sample answers:

9. As she puts words on paper, she can sort through what she is feeling and thinking. If she didn't have this escape valve, things would become overwhelming for her.

10. The foundation works to support women and children. Allende feels that women and children have the same rights as men. But often they are denied these rights. The foundation seeks to help women and children obtain the rights that are rightfully theirs.

Getting the Main Idea

Answers will vary. Sample answer:
Isabel Allende has overcome many difficulties in her life. She learned to work through her problems in a positive, constructive manner through her writing. She has worked hard all her life to achieve her goals and promote her ideas. She has used her wealth to improve the lives of needy women and children.

Applying What You've Learned

Answers will vary.

Mario Molina

Remembering the Facts

1. He received a toy microscope as a child and began doing experiments with it.

2. He learned that scientists in other places were using them to make weapons.

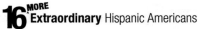

3. They were used as coolants in air conditioners and refrigerators. They were used as propellants in spray cans.

4. He wrote about his findings that CFCs were breaking down in the stratosphere and attacking the ozone layer.

5. He began a public awareness campaign. He wrote articles. He spoke on news programs. He spoke to business and government leaders about the problem.

6. He won for his discovery that CFCs were destroying the ozone layer.

7. He donated it to MIT to help students from poor countries come to the United States to study atmospheric chemistry.

8. a center to study energy and the environment

Understanding the Story

Answers will vary. Sample answers:

9. The ozone layer makes life on Earth possible. Without the ozone layer to protect plants and animals from the sun's UV rays, plants would die. People would get skin cancer and suffer other health problems. The result would eventually be catastrophic for life on Earth. Mario Molina's work made the world aware that it had to take steps to avert this threat.

10. There are many other sources of air pollution besides CFCs. One that Molina is concerned about today is pollution from fossil fuels.

Getting the Main Idea

Answers will vary. Sample answer:
Mario Molina is a role model because he focused his energy and worked toward his goals even when it meant he was isolated as a youth. When he made his breakthrough discoveries, he worked to make sure that people paid attention to them and made changes that were needed.

Applying What You've Learned

Answers will vary. They might include human-made sources such as power plants, factories, waste incinerators, motor vehicles, planes, ships, fireplaces, furnaces, oil refining, burning in agriculture or forestry management, fumes from solvents such as paints or hair sprays, waste in landfills, military sources such as nuclear weapons, toxic gases, and so on. They might also include natural sources such as dust, methane, radon gas, wildfires, and volcanic activity.

Bill Richardson

Remembering the Facts

1. His parents made sure that the children learned to speak both Spanish and English. The family celebrated the holidays of both countries.

2. His father insisted that he go to college instead.

3. Humphrey spoke about how he had dedicated his life to fighting poverty and injustice. He said he was proud that he could use his position to help his fellow citizens. Richardson realized that a person with a vision could change the world.

4. He represented the Third Congressional District of New Mexico.

5. He helped them protect their land and get better health care and better schools.

6. He was nominated because of his work in getting hostages released and his diplomatic efforts to end suffering around the world.

7. (any three) He created new jobs. He balanced the state budget. He secured a pay raise for teachers. He led the state to give health insurance to all children age five and younger. He oversaw an increase in the minimum wage. He led the state to provide life-insurance policies for National Guardsmen serving on active duty. He worked to make New Mexico the Clean Energy State.

8. New Mexico is a national leader in the wind, solar, and biofuel industries.

Understanding the Story

Answers will vary. Sample answers:

9. During his youth, Richardson felt out of place because he was both Mexican and American. He felt as if he didn't really fit in either world. As an adult, he used his diversity of experience to his advantage as he worked in politics.

10. Richardson learned to get along with people of different ethnic and socioeconomic backgrounds. He had a diverse, multi-cultural background.

Getting the Main Idea

Answers will vary. Sample answer:
Richardson has worked hard to support the causes he believes in. He has dedicated his life toward helping his fellow citizens achieve a better life.

Applying What You've Learned

Answers will vary.

Carlos Santana

Remembering the Facts

1. His father taught him starting at age five. Later, he took lessons at a local music college.

2. It is Mexican dance music played by small groups that include violins and trumpets.

3. Carlos had discovered the blues music of B. B. King and wanted to play the guitar like him.

4. Many new rock bands were forming in San Francisco. Also, the Fillmore Auditorium hosted great musicians who played many different kinds of music.

5. His playing brought half a million people to their feet. It was instant stardom.

6. He saw that many musicians were becoming burned out on drugs and a bad lifestyle. This included himself and some of his fellow band members. He felt that he had reached a dead end in his life.

7. Half of the music was done in the original Santana style. The other half consisted of duets with younger, popular musicians.

8. Its purpose is to raise money to help needy children around the world. It supports programs in the areas of health, education, and the arts.

Understanding the Story

Answers will vary. Sample answers:

9. His mother taught him to have a balanced perspective on life. His father taught him that serving our fellow people is the purpose of life. Thus, he was able to avoid some of the pitfalls that befell other musicians.

10. It has a strong Latin component. He plays beautiful blues-based guitar melodies. These are supported by strong Latin rhythms played on the conga drums or timbales.

Getting the Main Idea

Answers will vary. Sample answer:
Carlos Santana worked hard to make a name for himself in the world of music. At the same time, he kept the values he learned from his parents. He made family, service to others, and self-improvement the centers of his life. He has given his time and money to help those in need around the world.

Applying What You've Learned

Answers will vary.

Antonia Hernandez

Remembering the Facts

1. MALDEF, the Mexican American Legal Defense and Educational Fund

2. The other kids teased her. The teacher did not speak Spanish, and Antonia did not speak English.

3. She babysat her brothers and sisters. She sold tamales. She worked at produce stands. She worked picking crops in the summer.

4. She thought she could help the kids and teachers she worked with more by working to change the unfair laws that held back minorities.

5. She advised the committee on immigration and human-rights issues. She worked for voting rights and bilingual education.

6. (any three) fair funding for public schools; fair drawing of school-district lines; more jobs for Hispanics; fair drawing of voting districts; defeat of an I.D. bill; stopping nominations of federal judges with poor civil-rights records; defeat of Proposition 187; training Hispanics to sit on policy-making boards; training parents to be leaders in schools and advocate for their children; use of bilingual education

7. president and CEO of the California Community Foundation (CCF)

8. It works to improve the lives of poor people in Los Angeles. It connects those who wish to donate money with worthy causes that help people in need.

Understanding the Story

Answers will vary. Sample answers:

9. Some people do not wish to pay for bilingual education classes. Others think that the children should also be taught in their native language over a period of several years so that they will not fall behind in their schoolwork.

10. All minority groups have many issues in common. All may face discrimination in the workplace, in school, or in many other areas. They may be denied equal opportunities. By working together, they will have a stronger voice.

Getting the Main Idea

Answers will vary. Sample answer:
Antonia Hernandez is a role model because she has dedicated her life to helping the less fortunate.

Applying What You've Learned

Answers will vary.

Gloria Estefan
Remembering the Facts

1. Fidel Castro took over Cuba. He jailed or imprisoned former supporters of Fulgencio Batista. The family could no longer live there safely. No one would hire Gloria's father.

2. The purpose was to overthrow the communist government in Cuba. The U.S. government did not want a communist country only 90 miles away from Florida.

3. After serving in the Vietnam War, he became very ill. He was unable to care for himself.

4. It was the first song ever to appear on the Latin, R&B, and dance charts at the same time.

5. She was riding in a tour bus when a truck crashed into the bus.

6. (any two) They sent money to the United Way hurricane relief fund. They collected clothing. They organized a benefit concert. They donated the proceeds from the video "Always Tomorrow" to hurricane relief.

7. It is the highest honor given to a U.S. citizen who was not born in the United States.

8. It donates about half a million dollars a year to charity.

Understanding the Story

Answers will vary. Sample answers:

9. As a teenager, she wrote songs about her feelings as she cared for her ill father and younger sister. She found that writing the songs and then singing them was a good way to work out her feelings. She continued to do this during times of trouble, including after the bus accident.

10. Gloria's family escaped from Cuba. Estefan has been an outspoken opponent of the communist regime there throughout her life. She also sends this message in much of her music. The communist regime does not want the people of Cuba hearing this message.

Getting the Main Idea

Answers will vary. Sample answer:
Estefan has held fast to her values throughout her life. She has worked hard to overcome personal tragedy in her own life. She has also been a tireless worker on behalf of other people who are suffering loss. She started her life in the United States with nothing. Through hard work and determination, she and her husband have built an entertainment empire.

Applying What You've Learned

Answers will vary.

Edgar Prado

Remembering the Facts

1. His father was a trainer, and his two older brothers were jockeys.

2. He got his work ethic from her. She gave him a lot of support and made him the person he became.

3. He can communicate his affection to horses. He can quickly tell a horse's strengths, weaknesses, likes, and dislikes.

4. New York State is one of the largest horse-racing centers in the United States. He would have more opportunities there.

5. the Kentucky Derby

6. It is a series of three horse races: the Kentucky Derby, the Preakness Stakes, and the Belmont Stakes.

7. His right hind leg was broken in many places.

8. a lot of hard work and a lot of good horses to ride

Understanding the Story

Answers will vary. Sample answers:

9. Barbaro was a beautiful horse. He was big and muscular. He had extraordinary strength and endurance. When he won the Kentucky Derby by such a huge margin, he became a national hero. After his injury, people followed his recovery closely.

10. Jockeys can be involved in many types of accidents during a horse race or in training. They are often thrown from horses and may be trampled by other horses during a race.

Getting the Main Idea

Answers will vary. Sample answer:
Prado is a hard-working man who followed his dream to success. When he lost one race, he moved on to the next one. Even though his heart was broken by the loss of Barbaro, he continued his career.

Applying What You've Learned

Answers will vary.

Salma Hayek

Remembering the Facts

1. She became the most famous actress in Mexico.

2. Few movies were being made in Mexico.

3. Director Richard Rodriguez saw her on a talk show and was impressed with her.

4. She played a strong Mexican woman, a non-stereotyped role. The movie was a hit.

5. to provide chances for Hispanic actors, actresses, and other film-industry workers

6. *Frida*

7. Women should be valued for more than their looks.

8. She is a spokesperson for the foundation's Speak Out Against Domestic Violence program.

Understanding the Story

Answers will vary. Sample answers:

9. She talked her parents into sending her to a private school. She learned how to become an actress by working in local productions. She left a comfortable life in Mexico to go to Hollywood. She overcame a language barrier. She kept trying out for a part in a film. She formed her own production company. (Accept other reasonable answers.)

10. These actors and actresses may not have the confidence or determination needed to succeed in larger companies. Hayek's companies are smaller and can give them the attention and opportunities they need to succeed.

Getting the Main Idea

Answers will vary. Sample answer:
She has followed her dream with great determination and didn't give up when things got tough.

Applying What You've Learned

Answers will vary.

Christy Turlington

Remembering the Facts

1. She was a lot taller, and her hair was different.

2. A photographer spotted her horseback riding when she was a young teen. He thought she had potential as a model.

3. Traveling and doing modeling jobs was much more exciting.

4. She was the "face" of his advertising campaign for a fragrance called Eternity.

5. Many people in the modeling industry laughed at her. They thought she would not be smart enough for college.

6. She climbed Mt. Kilimanjaro in Africa.

7. She hopes to influence young women not to start smoking.

8. Yoga helps her keep her life in balance.

Understanding the Story

Answers will vary. Sample answers:

9. Models are exposed to a lifestyle that is prone to excess. Many people around them are very rich and famous. They may lead a jet-setting life of partying, drinking, wild spending, and so on. This would make it hard to focus on what's important in life. Models may be valued for what they look like and how much money they have rather than for their achievements or what they do to help others.

10. She has been able to keep herself focused on what is important. She is polite and professional, rather than difficult or demanding. She enjoyed the lifestyle of the rich and famous for a while, but then she realized that she was valued more for her looks than her personality. At this time, she had the courage to make a change in her life. She went to college and earned her degree. Then she focused much of her energy on doing charitable works.

Getting the Main Idea

Answers will vary. Sample answer:
Turlington has used her beauty and wealth to help others. She supports many charities that work for education, children, animal rights, and anti-tobacco campaigns.

Applying What You've Learned

Answers will vary.

Rebecca Lobo

Remembering the Facts

1. There were no professional teams for women. A woman would not be likely to be able to compete successfully on a men's team.

2. her long single braid

3. She scored 2,710 total points during her high-school career. She broke both the boys' and girls' records for high-school basketball in Massachusetts.

4. breast cancer

5. They won the national championship.

6. She won a gold medal as a member of the U.S. Olympic women's basketball team.

7. She was extremely popular with fans of all ages. Also, she was a good role model.

8. She suffered a knee injury in 1999 that never healed properly.

Understanding the Story

Answers will vary. Sample answers:

9. She was a very popular player. Her college games had been shown on national television and had good ratings and huge audiences. It seemed that the time was right to form some women's pro teams.

10. She chose children because she has a special bond with young children and they adore her. She works for breast cancer groups because of her mother's bout with that cancer. She supports education groups because she has always believed in the importance of education and was an excellent student herself.

Getting the Main Idea

Answers will vary. Sample answer:
Lobo tries to live her life in an exemplary way. She has always worked hard and done her very best. She kept perspective in her life and balanced school and basketball.

Applying What You've Learned

Answers will vary.

Alex Rodriguez

Remembering the Facts

1. He went to the after-school programs and joined the baseball team. He found a mentor in Eddie Rodriguez. He stayed off the streets.

2. He was an adult role model and like a father to Alex. He spent a lot of time with Alex. He drove Alex to baseball games.

3. It was a small school where he got a lot of attention. It also had one of the best baseball teams in the country.

4. He was just 18 years old and only one year out of high school.

5. It can be played year-round because of the climate. The teams compete on a high level.

6. 2003, 2005, 2007

7. He is a national spokesman for the group. He has donated his time and money. He pledged $500,000 to build an education center at the Miami club.

8. He donated $3.9 million to renovate the baseball field and to provide a four-year scholarship once a year to a graduate of the BGCA of Miami.

Understanding the Story

Answers will vary. Sample answers:

9. His mother was his strongest influence. He also had two good adult-male role models: his coach Eddie Rodriguez and Juan Arteaga.

10. A player might worry about a career-ending injury that could occur during the four college years before turning professional. The player might go professional for the money or fame. The player might not be strong academically. The player could go to college later in life.

Getting the Main Idea

Answers will vary. Sample answer:
Alex Rodriguez is a good role model because he worked very hard to gain his skills. Despite his fame and wealth, he has remained true to his values. He has donated time and money to give back to those organizations that supported him as a youth.

Applying What You've Learned

Answers will vary.

Scott Gomez

Remembering the Facts

1. Anchorage, Alaska

2. They organized raffles and pizza sales. They sold tacos at the Alaska State Fair.

3. New Jersey Devils

4. It is scoring three goals in one game.

5. 2000 and 2003

6. There was a contract dispute between the NHL players' association and the NHL. The NHL season was canceled.

7. He scored his 500th career point.

8. Its purpose is to advance the sport of youth hockey in Alaska. It seeks to support young players who need financial support so they can afford to play.

Understanding the Story

Answers will vary. Sample answers:

9. If there is more diversity among players, the NHL is likely to increase its fan base. Scott Gomez has been able to attract more Hispanic viewers, and more Hispanic youth to play the sport.

10. Hispanic Americans often live in states with warm climates such as Florida, Texas, California, and Arizona. Ice hockey is often not as popular there as in cold-climate states. The background of Hispanic Americans is also in countries where the climate is warm and hockey is less popular than soccer.

Getting the Main Idea

Answers will vary. Sample answer:
Gomez worked very hard to develop his skills in hockey and pursued his goal of playing in the NHL. He has used his position to advance the sport of hockey in his home state.

Applying What You've Learned

Answers will vary.

Additional Activities

Franklin Chang-Díaz

1. Read more about Ad Astra Rocket Company at www.adastrarocket.com. Report your findings to the class.

2. Learn more about other Hispanic Americans in NASA. Two of these are Ellen Ochoa and Carlos Noriega. Write a brief report on their contributions.

3. All of the space shuttles were named after sailing ships of the past. They are: *Enterprise* (earthbound test vehicle), *Columbia, Endeavour, Discovery, Atlantis,* and *Challenger.* Use the Internet to research one of them. Make a poster illustrating the shuttle you choose and listing important facts about it.

4. Use the Internet to research one of the Soviet space stations or the International Space Station. Report your findings to the class.

5. Report on another famous astronaut. Suggestions include the following:
   - Yuri Gagarin, the first person to enter space (1961)
   - Alan Shepard, the first American to enter space (1961)
   - John Glenn, the first American to orbit the earth (1962)
   - Neil Armstrong and Buzz Aldrin, the first men on the moon (1969)
   - Sally Ride, the first female U.S. astronaut (1983)

6. Use the Internet to research the work of Dr. Wernher von Braun, one of the first rocket pioneers.

7. Use the Internet to learn more about the disastrous flights of *Challenger* (1986) and *Columbia* (2003).

8. Research and report on the life of an astronaut in space. You might include eating, moving around, exercising, sleeping, bathroom and shower arrangements, and work.

Joseph Unanue

1. Go to your local grocery store and find the Goya section. Look at the array of Goya products. Make a list of three of these you would like to try. (If there is not a Goya section, ask the manager if the store sells any Goya products.)

2. Choose a recipe from the Goya Web site, www.goya.com. Explain your recipe to the class. Try making it at home.

3. Go to the Goya Web site and look at Goya's product line. Choose a product that you are unfamiliar with. Find out what it is and how it is used in cooking. Report your findings to the class.

Guy Gabaldon

1. Use the Internet to learn more about the Battle of Saipan.

2. Research what Saipan is like today. Make a travel poster illustrating one of its attractions. List other attractions below your drawing.

3. Watch the movie *Hell to Eternity* or the documentary *East L.A. Marine*.

4. In World War I, Sgt. Alvin C. York won fame for capturing a number of prisoners. Read about his story. Report to the class on what you learn.

5. Find out more about a Medal of Honor winner. Report to the class on what this person did to earn the Medal of Honor.

6. Use the Internet to learn more about another famous U.S. Marine. Report to the class about the person you chose.

Nicholasa Mohr

1. Learn more about one of the Mexican painters who inspired Mohr: Frida Kahlo, Diego Rivera, or José Clemente Orozco.

2. Obtain prints of some of the artwork of those Mexican painters and show them to the class.

3. Obtain prints of some of Nicholasa Mohr's artwork. Show these to the class.

4. Read one of Mohr's books. Give a brief report on your impressions of the book.

5. Use the Internet to research other famous Hispanic-American artists. Choose one to report on to the class.

6. Use the Internet to research other famous Hispanic-American writers. Choose one to report on to the class. Suggestions include Oscar Hijuelos, Gary Soto, Martin Espada, Sandra Cisneros, Rudolfo Anaya, and Julia Alvarez.

Isabel Allende

1. Learn more about the Isabel Allende Foundation at www.isabelallendefoundation.org.

2. Research the procedure a person who was not born in the United States would go through in order to become a U.S. citizen. (This is called the naturalization process.)

3. Read more about Salvador Allende and the overthrow of his government by Augusto Pinochet in 1973. Report your findings to the class.

4. Research feminist leaders such as Betty Friedan and Gloria Steinem.

5. Read one of Isabel Allende's novels. Make a poster to illustrate the main theme of the book.

Mario Molina

1. Read more about the hole in the ozone layer. Report your findings to the class.

2. The UV index tells you how much UV radiation there is on a given day. Make a poster illustrating how the UV index works. Include safety precautions to be taken at each level.

3. Research steps to take to keep safe in the sun. Make a poster showing these steps.

4. Popocatepetl is one of the most active volcanoes in Mexico. Use the Internet to research this volcano. Write a brief report about your findings.

5. Use the Internet to research an area affected by air pollution that interests you.

6. Use the Internet to make a list of ways lasers are used both for peaceful uses and as weapons.

7. Learn more about the Nobel Prize and its founder, Alfred Nobel. Report on your findings to the class.

8. Use the Internet to research CFCs. Make a poster showing how they were used and their effects on the atmosphere.

9. Use the Internet to make a list of the major sources of air pollution today.

10. Research the link between air pollution and global warming.

Bill Richardson

1. Use the Internet to research what Bill Richardson is doing today.

2. Use the Internet to learn more about the Energy and Commerce Committee of the U.S. House of Representatives. Make a list of the major responsibilities of this committee.

3. Research the Interior Committee of the U.S. House of Representatives. Make a list of the major responsibilities of this committee.

4. Make a poster about renewable energy. Include information on the basic sources of renewable power.

5. Make a time line illustrating the major events in the life of Bill Richardson.

Carlos Santana

1. Use the Internet to access Carlos Santana's official Web site at www.santana.com. It contains information about his life and his foundation.

2. Obtain a sample of Santana's music. Listen to it. Then play your favorite song(s) for the class. Point out the features of each song and explain why you like each one.

3. Visit the Web site of the Milagro Foundation at www.milagrofoundation.org. Make a poster or report showing some of the groups the foundation has supported.

4. Learn more about the San Francisco Mission District where Carlos lived as a young man at www.sfmission.com/santana.

5. Use the Internet to research the towns of Autlán de Navarro and Tijuana, Mexico. Draw a map of Mexico showing the locations of the towns. Write a short description of each town at the bottom of your map.

6. Learn more about mariachi music. Obtain a sample and play a mariachi song for the class.

7. Obtain a sample of any of the musical greats of the 1960s. Listen to the music and report your impressions to the class.

8. Use the Internet to research the Woodstock music festival. Make a poster advertising some of the bands that played at Woodstock.

Antonia Hernandez

1. Use the Internet to research bilingual education. Explain some of the different models commonly used to the class.

2. Use the Internet to learn more about MALDEF. Make a poster listing its main areas of effort.

3. Use the Internet to learn more about the CCF. Explain how the group helps those with money they wish to donate to a worthy cause connect with those in need.

Gloria Estefan

1. Listen to Gloria Estefan's music. Play some of your favorite songs for classmates.

2. Make a time line showing the important events in Estefan's life.

3. Use the Internet to research the Elian Gonzalez controversy that occurred in 2000.

4. Use the Internet to learn more about the Bay of Pigs invasion. Write a brief report on this incident.

5. Use the Internet to research the life of Fidel Castro, dictator of Cuba for many years.

6. Gloria's husband, Emilio Estefan, is an extraordinary Hispanic American as well. Learn more about his life. Report your findings to the class.

Edgar Prado

1. Use the Internet to learn about Prado's hometown, Lima, Peru. Make a travel poster to illustrate the attractions there.

2. Use the Internet to learn more about another famous jockey. Give a brief report on your findings to the class.

3. Use the Internet to research one of the major horse races, such as the Kentucky Derby, the Belmont Stakes, or the Preakness Stakes. Explain what you learn about these races to the class.

4. Use the Internet to learn more about the story of Barbaro. Make a poster illustrating the beautiful horse. Make a list of some facts about Barbaro under your drawing.

5. Use the Internet to research another famous racehorse. Some of these are Secretariat, Man o' War, and Seabiscuit.

6. Barbaro's injury and death have led to a debate over safety issues in thoroughbred horse racing. These issues include breeding horses for speed rather than durability, medication issues (use of steroids), and use of synthetic vs. dirt tracks. Choose one of these issues to report on to the class. You could also have a class debate on one or more of these issues.

Salma Hayek

1. Use the Internet to learn more about Hayek's birthplace: Coatzacoalcos, Veracruz, Mexico. Write a report or make a poster to illustrate the attractions of this area.

2. Watch one of Hayek's movies. Report your impressions to the class.

3. Use the Internet to learn more about director Robert Rodriguez or actor Antonio Banderas. Report on your findings to the class.

4. Learn more about the Avon Foundation's program against domestic violence, partnered with Hayek, at www.avoncompany.com/women/speakout.

5. Learn more about the 1 Pack = 1 Vaccine program at www.unicefusa.org/news/releases/salma-hayek-joins-with.html.

Christy Turlington

1. Use the Internet to learn more about PETA. Give a report on one of the current projects of this group.

2. Use the Internet to learn more about the American Cancer Society. Make a poster showing the mission and activities of this group.

3. Learn more about the practice of yoga. Report your findings to the class.

4. Use the Internet to learn about another famous model. Give a brief report on this person's work.

5. Visit Turlington's antismoking Web site at www.smokingisugly.com. Report to the class on something you learn from the site.

Rebecca Lobo

1. Watch a WNBA game on television. Report on the game to the class.

2. Use the Internet to research another women's basketball star. Examples include Cheryl Miller, Sheryl Swoopes, Teresa Edwards, Katrina McClain, and Lisa Leslie. Write a brief report on the person you chose.

3. Use the Internet to find out more about Lobo's career today.

4. Choose a team in the WNBA. Report on its season to the class.

Alex Rodriguez

1. Use the Internet to make a list of other famous Hispanic-American baseball players.

2. Make a word web to describe Alex Rodriguez.

3. Make a graph to illustrate Rodriguez's home-run record throughout his career.

4. Find out more about the Boys & Girls Clubs of America. Report on your findings to the class. See if there is a BGCA group in your town.

5. Use the Internet to make a list of other major-league players from the Dominican Republic or of Dominican descent.

6. Make a poster illustrating Alex Rodriguez's baseball statistics.

7. Tune in to one of Rodriguez's games and watch him play. Write a story about the game.

8. Learn more about Alex Rodriguez by visiting his official Web site at http://arod.mlb.com/players/rodriguez_alex/index.jsp.

9. Use the Web site listed above to learn more about the AROD Family Foundation.

Scott Gomez

1. Learn more about the Scotty Gomez Foundation at www.scottygomezfoundation.com.

2. Use the Internet to learn more about Scott Gomez's career.

3. Use the Internet to read more about another famous hockey player. Examples include Wayne Gretzky, Mark Messier, Brett Hull, Bobby Orr, and Claude Lemieux.

4. Learn more about the rules of hockey. Explain the game to the class.

5. Use the Internet to research the Stanley Cup. Write a brief report on its origins and history.

References

Franklin Chang-Díaz

Ad Astra Rocket Company Web site. www.adastrarocket.com.

Astronaut Bio: Franklin Chang-Díaz. NASA Web site. www.jsc.nasa.gov/Bios/htmlbios/chang.html.

D'Agnese, Joseph. "Space Explorer: Franklin Chang-Díaz." *Discover Magazine.* November 8, 2003. http://discovermagazine.com/2003/nov/space-explorer.

"Franklin Chang-Díaz." *Contemporary Hispanic Biography,* Vol. 2. Farmington Hills, MI: Gale Group, 2002. Reproduced in *Biography Resource Center.* Farmington Hills, MI: Gale, 2008. http://galenet.galegroup.com/servlet/BioRc.

Pedrero, Wendy. "The Sky's the Limit for Latinos in NASA: Unbeknownst to the Hispanic Community's Mainstream, There Are Plenty of Latino Heroes Pushing the Envelope in Space Exploration." *Latino Leaders,* October-November 2004, pp. 22–25.

Spangenburg, Ray, and Kit Moser. *Onboard the Space Shuttle.* New York: Franklin Watts, 2002.

Joseph Unanue

DeLollis, Barbara. "CEO Profile: At Goya, It's All in la Familia." *USA Today,* March 24, 2008. www.usatoday.com/money/companies/management/2008-03-23-bob-unanue-goya-foods-N.htm.

Demetrakakes, Pan. "Hispanic Consumers Are Goya's Gold Mine: The No. 1 Food Company Among U.S. Hispanics Reflects Tradition in Both Products and Packaging." *Food & Drug Packaging,* August 2003. http://findarticles.com.

Denker, Joel. *The World on a Plate: A Tour Through the History of America's Ethnic Cuisine.* Boulder, CO: Westview Press, 2003.

Goya Foods Web site. www.goya.com.

"Joseph A. Unanue." Ellis Island Medals of Honor Web site. www.neco.org/awards/recipients/josephaunanue.html.

"Joseph A. Unanue." www.en.wikipedia.org/wiki/Joseph_A._Unanue.

Snyder, Jennifer, and Jose Delanoy. "Goya Foods, Inc. Collection." December 2001. http://americanhistory.si.edu/archives/d7694.htm.

U.S. Latino and Latina World War II Oral History Project Web site. www.lib.utexas.edu/ww2latinos.

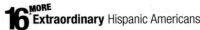

Guy Gabaldon

"The Battle of Saipan." http://www.navysite.de/ships/lha2about.htm.

Goldstein, Richard. "Guy Gabaldon, 80, Hero of Battle of Saipan, Dies." www.nytimes.com/2006/09/04/us/04gabaldon.html.

"Guy Gabaldon." http://en.wikipedia.org/wiki/Guy_Gabaldon.

"Guy Gabaldon: An Interview and Discussion." *The War Times Journal.* www.wtj.com/articles/gabaldon.

Guy Gabaldon's Web site. www.guygabaldon.com.

Kakesako, Gregg K. "'Pied Piper' Returning to Saipan." *The Honolulu Star-Bulletin.* June 6, 2004. http://archives.starbulletin.com/2004/06/06/news/story10.html.

Lin, Lynda. "A Friendship Like No Other." *Pacific Citizen,* October 20, 2006. www.pacificcitizen.org/content/2006/national/oct20-lin-friendship.htm.

Nicholasa Mohr

Barbato, Joseph. "Latino Writers in the American Market." *Publishers Weekly,* February 1, 1991, pp. 17–21. www.galenet.galegroup.com/servlet/BioRC.

Erlich, Amy, ed. *When I Was Your Age,* Vol. 1. Cambridge, MA: Candlewick Press, 1996.

Mohr, Nicholasa. *Growing Up Inside the Sanctuary of My Imagination.* New York: Simon & Schuster, 1995.

"Nicholasa Mohr." *Contemporary Hispanic Biography,* Vol. 2. Farmington Hills, MI: Gale Group, 2002. Reproduced in *Biography Resource Center.* Farmington Hills, MI: Gale, 2008. http://galenet.galegroup.com/servlet/BioRC.

"Nicholasa Mohr." *Major Authors and Illustrators for Children and Young Adults,* 2nd ed. Farmington Hills, MI: Gale Group, 2002. Reproduced in *Biography Resource Center.* Farmington Hills, MI: Gale, 2008. http://galenet.galegroup.com/servlet/BioRC.

"Nicholasa Mohr." http://www2.scholastic.com/browse/contributor.jsp?id=3398.

"Nicholasa Mohr." www.balkinbuddies.com/mohr.

Isabel Allende

Allende, Isabel. *Paula: A Memoir.* New York: HarperCollins Publishers, 1994.

Allende, Isabel. *The Sum of Our Days: A Memoir.* New York: HarperCollins Publishers, 2008.

"Isabel Allende." *Contemporary Hispanic Biography,* Vol. 1. Farmington Hills, MI: Gale Group, 2002. Reproduced in *Biography Resource Center.* Farmington Hills, MI: Gale, 2008. http://galenet.galegroup.com/servlet/BioRC.

Isabel Allende Foundation Web site. www.isabelallendefoundation.org.

Isabel Allende's Web site. www.isabelallende.com/.

Main, Mary. *Isabel Allende: Award-Winning Latin American Author.* Berkeley Heights, NJ: Enslow Publishers, 2005.

Mario Molina

Kent, Deborah. *Mario Molina: Chemist and Nobel Prize Winner.* Chanhassen, MN: The Child's World, 2004.

"The Legend of Popocatépetl and Iztaccíhuatl" at "Popocatépetl." http://en.wikipedia.org/wiki/Popocatépetl.

"Mario Molina." *Scientists: Their Lives and Works,* Vols. 1–7. Online Edition, 2006. Reproduced in *Biography Resource Center.* Farmington Hills, MI: Gale, 2008. http://galenet.galegroup.com/servlet/BioRC.

Molina, Mario J. "Autobiography." http://nobelprize.org.nobel_prizes/chemistry/laureates/1995/molina-autobio.html.

Nemecek, Sasha. "Rescuing the Ozone Layer." *Scientific American,* November 1997, p. 40.

Bill Richardson

"Bill Richardson." *Current Biography.* The H.W. Wilson Company/Wilson Web. http://vnweb.hwwilsonweb.com.

Bill Richardson for President Web site. www.richardsonforpresident.com.

Richardson, Bill. *Between Worlds: The Making of an American Life.* New York: G.P. Putnam's Sons, 2005.

"Sources: Bill Richardson withdrawing as Cabinet nominee" CNN.com. http://www.cnn.com/2009/POLITICS/01/04/richardson.withdrawal/index.html.

Carlos Santana

Hedegaard, Erik. "Carlos' Cosmic Bummer." *Rolling Stone.* Oct. 16, 2008. http://www.rollingstone.com/news/story/23356489/carlos_cosmic_bummer.

"Carlos Santana." *Contemporary Hispanic Biographies,* Vol. 1. Farmington Hills, MI: Gale Group, 2002. Reproduced in *Biography Resource Center.* Farmington Hills, MI: Gale, 2008. http://galenet.galegroup.com/servlet/BioRC

"Carlos Santana." *Contemporary Musicians,* Vol. 43. Farmington Hills, MI: Gale Group, 2004. Reproduced in *Biography Resource Center.* Farmington Hills, MI: Gale, 2008. http://galenet.galegroup.com/servlet/BioRC

Carlos Santana's Web site. www.santana.com.

Milagro Foundation Web site. www.milagrofoundation.org.

Santana, Deborah. *Space Between the Stars: My Journey to an Open Heart.* New York: Ballantine, 2005.

Slavicek, Louise Chipley. *Carlos Santana.* New York: Chelsea House, 2006.

Woog, Adam. *Carlos Santana: Legendary Guitarist.* Farmington Hills, MI: Lucent Books, 2006.

Antonia Hernandez

"Antonia Hernandez."
http://gale.cengage.com/free_resources/chh/bio/hernandez_a.htm.

California Community Foundation Web site. www.calfund.org.

Enright, Elizabeth. "Antonia Hernandez, Civil Rights Activist." *AARP SegundaJuventud,* February/March 2005. www.aarpsegundajuventud.org/english/presence/2005-FM/05FM_Antonia_Hernandez.html.

MALDEF Web site. www.maldef.org.

"Raising the Bar: Pioneers in the Legal Profession—Antonia Hernandez." www.abanet.org/publiced/hernandez.html.

Gloria Estefan

"Gloria Estefan." *Contemporary Hispanic Biography,* Vol. 1. Farmington Hills, MI: Gale Group, 2002. Reproduced in *Biography Resource Center.* Farmington Hills, MI: Gale, 2008. http://galenet.galegroup.com/servlet/BioRC.

Gloria Estefan's Web site. http://www.gloriaestefan.com/cms/.

Lee, Sally. *Gloria Estefan: Superstar of Song.* Berkeley Heights, NJ: Enslow Publishers, 2005.

Legacy Recordings Gloria Estefan Web site. http://www.gloriaonline.com.

Parish, James Robert. *Gloria Estefan: Singer.* New York: Infobase Publishing, 2006.

Edgar Prado

"Edgar Prado." *Current Biography Yearbook 2007.* New York: The H.W. Wilson Co., September 2007, pp. 400–403.

McMurray, Jeffrey. "Study Finds 5,000 Horse Deaths at U.S. Tracks Since '03." Associated Press wire story, June 14, 2008. http://abcnews.go.com/Sports/wireStory?id=5132731.

Pedulla, Tom. "Prado's Perserverance." *USA Today,* May 16, 2006, p. 01C.

Philbin, Tom, and Pamela K. Brodowsky. *Barbaro: A Nation's Love Story.* New York: HarperCollins Publishers, 2007.

Prado, Edgar, with John Eisenberg. *My Guy Barbaro: A Jockey's Journey Through Love, Triumph, and Heartbreak with America's Favorite Horse.* New York: HarperCollins Publishers, 2008.

Simon, Scott. "Jockey Remembers 'My Guy Barbaro.'" *Weekend Edition* interview, May 3, 2008. www.npr.org/templates/story/story.php?storyid=90157350.

Salma Hayek

Avon Foundation Web site. www.avoncompany.com/women/speakout.

"Salma Hayek." *Contemporary Hispanic Biography,* Vol. 2. Farmington Hills, MI: Gale Group, 2002. Reproduced in *Biography Resource Center,* Farmington Hills, MI: Gale, 2008. http://galenet.galegroup.com/servlet/BioRC.

"Salma Hayek." http://en.wikipedia.org/wiki/Salma_Hayek.

"Salma Hayek." http://gale.cengage.com/free_resources/chh/bio/hayek_s.htm.

Scott, Kieran. *Salma Hayek.* Philadelphia: Chelsea House Publishers, 2001.

Valdez-Rodriguez, Alisa. "Salma Hayek." *Redbook,* November 2006, pp. 122–25.

Christy Turlington

"Christy Turlington." *Newsmakers,* Issue 4. Farmington Hills, MI: Gale Group, 2001. Reproduced in *Biography Resource Center,* Farmington Hills, MI: Gale, 2008. http://galenet.galegroup.com/servlet/BioRC.

"Christy Turlington." *Notable Hispanic American Women,* Book 2. Farmington Hills, MI: Gale Research, 1998. Reproduced in *Biography Resource Center.* Farmington Hills, MI: Gale, 2008. http://galenet.galegroup.com/servlet/BioRC.

Gross, Michael. "Beyond Super." *The Evening Standard,* July 7, 2006, p. 31. http://galenet.galegroup.com/servlet/BioRC.

Seeber, Michael. "Christy Turlington: Beauty and Balance." http://psychologytoday.com/articles.

Smoking Is Ugly Web site. www.smokingisugly.com.

Turlington, Christy. *Living Yoga: Creating a Life Practice.* New York: Hyperion, 2002.

Rebecca Lobo

Lobo, RuthAnn, and Rebecca Lobo. *The Home Team: Of Mothers, Daughters, and American Champions.* Kodansha International, 1996.

"Rebecca Lobo." *Contemporary Hispanic Biography,* Vol. 3. Farmington Hills, MI: Gale Group, 2003. Reproduced in *Biography Resource Center.* Farmington Hills, MI: Gale Group, 2003. http://galenet.galegroup.com/servlet/BioRC.

"Rebecca Lobo." *Current Biography Yearbook.* New York: The H.W. Wilson Co., 1997.

Rebecca Lobo's Web site. www.wnba.com/rebeccalobo.

Savage, Jeff. *Rebecca Lobo.* Berkeley Heights, NJ: Enslow Publishers, 2001.

Alex Rodriguez

"Alex Emmanuel Rodriguez." *Notable Sports Figures,* 4 vols. Farmington Hills, MI: Gale Group, 2004. Reproduced in *Biography Resource Center.* Farmington Hills, MI: Gale, 2008. http://galenet.galegroup.com/servlet/BioRC.

"Alex Rodriguez." *Contemporary Hispanic Biography,* Vol. 2. Farmington Hills, MI: Gale Group, 2002. Reproduced in *Biography Resource Center.* Farmington Hills, MI: Gale Group, 2008. http://galenet.galegroup.com/servlet/BioRC.

"Alex Rodriguez." http://gale.cengage.com/free_resources/chh/bio/rodriguez_alex.htm.

"Alex Rodriguez." *Newsmakers,* Issue 2. Farmington Hills, MI: Gale Group, 2001. Reproduced in *Biography Resource Center.* Farmington Hills, MI: Gale, 2008. http://galenet.galegroup.com/servlet.BioRC.

"Alex Rodriguez." The New York Yankees Web site. http://newyorkyankees.com.

Alex Rodriguez Web site. http://arod.mlb.com/players/rodriguez_alex/index.jsp

Christopher, Matt. *On the Field with ... Alex Rodriguez.* Boston: Little, Brown and Company, 2002.

Macnow, Glen. *Alex Rodriguez.* Berkeley Heights, NJ: Enslow Publishers, 2002.

Scott Gomez

"Mexican Ice Storm." http://hol.hispaniconline.com/HispanicMag/2007_2/Feature-ScottGomez.html.

O'Shei, Tim, and Amy Moritz. *Scott Gomez.* Philadelphia: Chelsea House Publishers, 2001.

"Scott Gomez." *Contemporary Hispanic Biography,* Vol. 2. Farmington Hills, MI: Gale Group, 2002. Reproduced in *Biography Resource Center.* Farmington Hills, MI: Gale Group, 2008. http://galenet.galegroup.com/servlet/BioRC.

"Scott Gomez." http://en.wikipedia.org/wiki/Scott_Gomez.

Scotty Gomez Foundation. www.scottygomezfoundation.com.

Stewart, Mark. *Scott Gomez: Open Up the Ice.* Brookfield, CT: The Millbrook Press, 2001.

WALCH EDUCATION
extending and enhancing learning

Let's stay in touch!

Thank you for purchasing these Walch Education materials. Now, we'd like to support you in your role as an educator. **Register now** and we'll provide you with updates on related publications, online resources, and more. You can register online at www.walch.com/newsletter, or fill out this form and fax or mail it to us.

Name _____ Date _____

School name _____

School address_____

City _____ State _____ Zip _____

Phone number (home) _____ (school) _____

E-mail _____

Grade level(s) taught _____ Subject area(s) _____

Where did you purchase this publication? _____

When do you primarily purchase supplemental materials? _____

What moneys were used to purchase this publication?

[　] School supplemental budget

[　] Federal/state funding

[　] Personal

[　] Please sign me up for Walch Education's free quarterly e-newsletter, *Education Connection.*

[　] Please notify me regarding free *Teachable Moments* downloads.

[　] Yes, you may use my comments in upcoming communications.

COMMENTS _____

_____

_____

_____

Please FAX this completed form to 888-991-5755, or mail it to:

Customer Service, Walch Education, 40 Walch Drive, Portland, ME 04103